306.81 Ant
Anthony, Carmen.
Getting married after 40
~~5-99~~

Getting Married After 40

Getting Married After 40

Advice & Inspiration from 100 Women Who Found Good Men & Happy Marriages

Carmen Anthony

MONTROSE LIBRARY DISTRICT
320 So. 2nd St.
Montrose, CO 81401

Adams Media Corporation
Holbrook, Massachusetts

Dedication

To my husband, Jerry Maher, with love.

Acknowledgments

I would like to thank my agent and friend, Linda Konner, for all the help she gave me on this book and for believing in me. I would also like to thank the International Women's Writing Guild (IWWG) for their wonderful writing seminars and their encouragement.

Copyright ©1999, Carmen Anthony. All rights reserved.This book, or parts thereof, may not be reproduced in any form without permission from the publisher; exceptions are made for brief excerpts used in published reviews.

Published by
Adams Media Corporation
260 Center Street, Holbrook, MA 02343

ISBN: 1-58062-115-5

Printed in the United States of America

J I H G F E D C B A

Library of Congress Cataloging-in-Publication Data
Anthony, Carmen.
Getting married after forty / by Carmen Anthony.
p. cm.
ISBN 1-58062-115-5
1. Middle aged women—United States—Interviews. 2. Married women—United States—Interviews. 3. Marriage—United States. I. Title. II. Marriage after forty.
HQ1059.5.U5A57 1999
305.244—dc21 98-31837
CIP

This publication is designed to provide accurate and authoritative information with regard to the subject matter covered. It is sold with the understanding that the publisher is not engaged in rendering legal, accounting, or other professional advice. If legal advice or other expert assistance is required, the services of a competent professional person should be sought.

— From a *Declaration of Principles* jointly adopted by a Committee of the American Bar Association and a Committee of Publishers and Associations

Cover photo by Raphael Junneau/FPG International.

This book is available at quantity discounts for bulk purchases.
For information, call 1-800-872-5627 (in Massachusetts, 781-767-8100).

Visit our home page at http://www.adamsmedia.com

Table of Contents

Introduction

In 1992 I did something that changed my life—something considered so unusual that women frequently give me a wide-eyed look and ask,

"How did you do it?"

"What's your secret?"

What did I do? Did I make $20 million in a real estate deal? Land a starring role on Broadway? Beam myself across town? Not quite. I did something many women apparently find equally miraculous: I exchanged wedding vows at age 52.

It's surprising how often I meet women who can't believe that someone over 40, let alone 50, could find a husband.

Although this is my second marriage (my first one ended in divorce when I was in my late 20s), I enjoyed the single life for some twenty-five years, with no children and no desire to have any. And then one evening, lightning struck. I met a wonderful man, and eventually I found myself at the Marriage Bureau again. I was delighted, but I didn't consider it any kind of miracle.

Olé

I met my second husband, Jerry, at a bullfight club in New York, where I'd been a member for six years. The club is an assortment of Hemingway types who follow the bullfights in Spain and Latin

America. My husband-to-be, a bullfight aficionado, heard about the club and dropped in at one of our monthly dinner meetings.

For him, it was love at first sight—love for the club, that is. He was too busy talking about matadors and picadors to notice me. But I wasn't offended—it's not easy finding bullfight enthusiasts in the heart of New York City. Eventually he did surface from all the taurine talk and introduced himself. A month later we had a dinner date. Three years later we were married.

"Boy, were you lucky!"

When I heard that for the umpteenth time, I decided I wanted to do something to help change older women's attitudes about themselves, to help them thumb their noses at statistics and all the naysayers and to start thinking positively about their chances of finding a good man. That's when I began the research that eventually led to this book. First I searched bookshelves and the Internet to see what type of material was available on older women and marriage. What I found were about a half dozen books on older marriages, most of them written by therapists. Lots of good advice, to be sure, but nothing from women themselves.

I wanted to write a woman-to-woman book, with advice from those who've been there to those who want to be there. That's when I decided to find other women who were 40 or older when they wed (or rewed) to see if there was anything about them that set them apart from women who wanted to marry but couldn't seem to connect with good men.

Is there a special type? Are there any patterns, any "secrets" that help define these women? To find out, I put together a questionnaire (see Appendix for sample), then placed ads in newspapers and notices in newsletters, and told everyone I knew about my project. Women from all over the country responded. I sent them the questionnaire and later followed up with telephone interviews.

It's About Time!

Many returned the questionnaire with enthusiastic, handwritten comments, such as, "It's about time someone told our story," or, "It's great to see a positive approach, for a change."

The women in this survey, whom I call the Marriage 100, ranged in age from 40 to 73 when they began their current marriage. More than 60 percent were in their 40s when they wed, about 25 percent were in their 50s, 10 percent were in their 60s, and one was 73. Slightly more than half are in their second marriage. Those in their first or third marriage are about evenly divided, and there's a sprinkling of colorful, never-say-die types who've gone to the altar four and five times.

Their stories are as varied as their backgrounds. Some of the stories are charming, such as the playwright in her late 60s who met her second husband at her first husband's funeral; or unorthodox, such as the woman who married her son's best friend. Most, however, are about women who met their husbands in fairly common ways—through personal ads, blind dates, on the job, or simply going along doing whatever interested them.

What I learned is this: If there's a common denominator among these 100 women, it's their eagerness to help dispel the notion that good men are hard to find when you're over 40 and that the older you get, the harder it gets. Virtually all of them had this to say to any mature woman who wants to find a good man:

DO be open and receptive to meeting new people.

DON'T think you're ever too old to enjoy a new relationship.

Although this is not a scientific survey, it does poll a diverse group of women and interesting patterns do emerge, making it possible to draw some broad conclusions that, hopefully, you can relate to and use in your own quest for finding the right man.

This book is a collection of the insights and opinions of 100 women who were willing to answer highly personal questions on everything from how they met their husbands to their sex lives; they also offer advice to single women and their views on the pros and cons of mature marriages. The questionnaire is primarily composed of open-ended questions. I did follow-up telephone interviews with a third of the Marriage 100 to probe more deeply into some of the issues they indicated they wanted to discuss. Many wrote out such long, detailed answers to my questions that phone calls weren't necessary. The women are real people and their stories are true; only their names have been changed to protect their privacy.

This is a book of sharing and caring, offered in the hope that some of the stories and insights will help guide other women to good men and happy marriages.

Chapter 1

Meet the Marriage 100

A woman goes mad twice—when she loves and when she begins to go grey.

—Polish proverb

Meet the Marriage 100, a tiny fraction of the hundreds of thousands of women who each year beat the so-called marriage odds. These women come in many sizes, shapes, religions, and ethnic groups. They're from every region of the country, from major metropolitan areas to small towns and farming centers. Some live in wealthy communities with swimming pools and tennis courts; others, in trailer parks or modest homes in working class neighborhoods, and still others, in high-rise apartments in New York, or condos in Florida. Some are professional women, others are homemakers. Many have children from previous marriages, many are stepmothers, some are grandmothers.

Everyday Types

These women have one thing in common: All of them were 40 or older when they exchanged wedding vows—all of them wed men who were *not* looking for babes or teenyboppers.

Several are free spirits who paid little heed to the opinions of others and never even considered their age as an obstacle to meeting men. Most, however, have had their share of fears and doubts about getting older and being alone.

For some, those fears hit home the day they took stock of the grey in their hair, the closets full of skirts and slacks with elastic waistbands, and the sags here and there. If they weren't already in a relationship, many had that sinking feeling that they'd probably never be in one again. Some didn't care, of course, but they're in the minority. Many bought into the belief that if you're over 40, you're over the hill, at least as far as finding a good man is concerned.

Yet these 100 women *did* find husbands, and they're here to show you that what they did is not as difficult or as unusual as you may think. In subsequent chapters we're going to find out what they have to say about older marriages in general, and their marriages in particular. They're going to hand out advice (whether or not it was advice they themselves followed), and they're going to express many different points of view. Undoubtedly, you'll agree with some and disagree with others.

You'll see how they resolved problems that could be bothering you, hear some entertaining stories that might relate to your own life, gain some insights and, hopefully, come away feeling good about your own marriage prospects. As one woman said, "If I can do it, anyone can do it."

Just the Facts, Ma'am

Age

Here are some characteristics of the Marriage 100 that illustrate the diversity of the group.

- 66 were in their 40s when they wed their current husband.
- 24 were in their 50s.
- 9 were in their 60s.
- 1 was in her 70s.

Number of Marriages

- 19 are in their first marriage.
- 57 are in their second marriage.
- 22 are in their third marriage.
- 1 is in her fourth marriage.
- 1 is in her fifth marriage.

Number of Children

- 69 have children from previous marriages.
- 55 of the 69 wed men with children.
- 15 do not have children, but married men with children.
- 14 do not have children and neither do their husbands.
- 11 have children and married men who do not have children.
- 38 have grandchildren.
- 2 have a child with their current husband.
- 13 have children or stepchildren who were living at home at the time of their current marriage.

Sound Familiar?

As you get to know these women, you'll see that their lives and attitudes drive home the point that there are no hard and fast rules when it comes to dating and mating. For every woman who thinks you only meet "losers" at singles parties, there's at least one woman who met her husband at a singles event. For every woman who hates blind dates, the bar scene, or personal ads, there's one who'll tell you that's how she met her husband. Listen to what these 100 women have to say, take what works for you, and ignore the rest.

First, let's get acquainted with Barbara, Helen, and Dolores, and see if any of their comments sound familiar:

When Barbara turned 40 her life was full, but, "I was single and very much aware that time had run out. That meant no children, no one to grow old with."

Helen, a twice-divorced single mother in her 40s, had an active social life with plenty of friends, but, "I wondered if I'd ever marry again. I was getting to the point where I told myself it didn't matter. Having been married twice before, I was afraid of making a mistake a third time."

Dolores, a widow in her 60s, was lonely being on her own after a 31-year marriage, "I wasn't going out much. You can get into so much trouble doing that, going to places where you don't need to be going to, and looking for someone."

All of these women eventually married good men. Barbara met her husband through a singles group; Helen, through work; and Dolores, through church. We'll hear more from them later. But before we go any further, let's examine why so many mature women feel age is a handicap in the marriage market.

What 40 Looks Like

When Gloria Steinem turned 40 and people remarked that she didn't look 40, she said words to the effect that, "This is what 40 looks like, if women would stop lying about their age." Ten years later, on turning 50, she made the same assertion.

Unfortunately, many prominent women lack her candor. Even most glamour queens who admit to being over 40 or even 50, have had extensive plastic surgery to look younger, not to mention the services of top-dollar makeup artists and hair coloring specialists.

The beauty and fashion industries don't help much either. With their emphasis on youth, thinness, perfect teeth, and flawless complexions, they can make even the most attractive woman feel old and dumpy. We know, of course, that many of those cover girls with the baby-smooth skin are just that: *girls*. Some are as young as 11 or 12, made up to look older. The fashion spreads, the ads for perfumes and beauty products, cruise lines, jewelry—you name it—almost always feature very young women, even if the products they promote are for older women. Presumably, women want to fantasize about looking as good as the models if they buy the products (and men just want to fantasize).

Then there are the love stories in movies and on TV, almost always involving young, beautiful women (but not necessarily young, gorgeous men). Where is the female equivalent of Andy Sipowicz, he of the bald head and big gut in *NYPD Blue*, who lands the beautiful, sexy mate late in life?

Terrorists or Wedding Bells?

It didn't help much when *Newsweek* declared in a 1986 cover story that a 40-year-old woman has a greater chance of being kidnapped by terrorists than of finding a husband. "Too Late for Prince Charming?" asked the headline from hell, which, more than a dozen years later, continues to resonate among single women. The article was a report on "Marriage Patterns in the United States," a demographics study by three Ivy League sociologists. Their findings showed, among other things, that college-educated women still single at 35 have only a five percent chance of ever getting married, and 40-year-old women, a minuscule 2.6 percent chance. That led *Newsweek*, not the sociologists, to conclude that these women were more apt to meet up with terrorists than hear wedding bells.

Judging from the intense media coverage, the spin-off articles, and the talk show prattle, the story triggered panic attacks in single women from coast to coast. It sounded as if the only thing worse that could befall these poor, unmarried creatures was standing next to a nuclear reactor during meltdown. What so many people lost sight of during all the hype, was that the findings failed to take into account the fact that many educated women put off marriage while they pursue careers, and many others *choose* not to marry at all. The sociologists themselves said they were dealing with statistical averages, not individual odds.

Even though the article was published in 1986, virtually all of the Marriage 100 remembered the article or had heard about it. And, more than ten years later, just about every one of them was familiar with the comment about terrorists, whether or not they knew the source. While not all of them bought into the article's premise, the fact that so many remember it indicates that negative views of the marriage prospects of women of a "certain age" still run deep and wide.

Following are some comments on the subject from the Marriage 100.

So What!

- "I thought the concept was ridiculous, but it still struck terror somewhere deep inside."—Legal administrator, wed for the third time at 40 to an executive she met in her firm.
- It was frightening. That was the year I was getting divorced. I figured I'd never marry again, so I set about having a happy life anyway."—Publicist, wed for the second time at 45 to a land developer she met in an elevator.
- "It took a lot of women's hope away. In order for something to happen, one has to believe that it's possible. The hopeful lost hope and the cynical were validated."—Hair stylist, wed for the third time at 50 to a businessman she met in a personal growth workshop.
- "I wondered, should I panic?"—Paralegal, wed for the third time at 57 to a structural engineer she met on a blind date.
- "So what! It's only for those who feel a woman needs to be married to be happy and fulfilled."—Emergency room nurse, wed for the second time at 40 to a doctor she met on the job.

How Bad Is It?

> *I've known lots of women who were well over 40 when they wed, I don't know anyone who was kidnapped by terrorists.*
>
> —A saleswoman who wed for the third time at 61 to a marketing executive she met at a singles party.

They say your chances of being struck by lightning are 500,000 to 1. But what does that really mean? When lightning strikes don't the odds of being hit change if you're on a lake holding a metal fishing rod, or on a golf course swinging a club, or standing under a tree? And what are the odds if, like the vast majority of people, you run for cover at the first sign of trouble and are safely ensconced in a building when lightning strikes, not to mention the millions who weren't outside in the first place. Are these 500,000 to 1 odds as true for people who live in the desert as for those who live in tropical climates? In other words, if you throw everyone into the same equation, aren't you going to end up with an average that doesn't really mean much? Remember, whether we're talking lightning strikes or marriage chances, you're not an average, you're not a statistic, you're an individual with choices.

When it comes to published marriage statistics, just how bad is it for the older woman? Depressing, to say the least, *if* you only look at the percentages or averages. But look at total numbers and you'll get a different perspective.

First, the bad news. In a special study released in 1991 through its publication, *Monthly Vital Statistics Report*, the National Center for Health Statistics (NCHS), which tracks marriages in this country, reported that in 1988 (the latest date for which figures are available) single women ages 20–24 were five times as likely to marry as single women 40–44, and 34 times as likely to marry as single women 60–64.

Now the good news, and there's plenty of it. According to other figures compiled by the NCHS, well over a quarter-million women age 40 and older exchanged wedding vows in 1992, and the figure was just under a quarter-million for 1982. (The exact numbers are 274,519 for 1992 and 228,466 for 1982, and that is bound to increase as more and more baby boomers turn 40 and 50.)

Isn't what's possible for one woman, let alone a quarter-million, possible for you?

The marriage number for men over 40 was higher—388,403 for 1992 and 341,650 for 1982. Isn't it a safe bet that many of them married women in their own age group?

If you still think that you've a greater chance of being struck by lightning on a cloudless day in the middle of a busy street than of finding a good man, then it's time to take a look at the Marriage 100, women who refused to think of themselves as statistics and created their own favorable odds.

First of all, they will tell you to get an attitude, but make it a positive one. In one way or another, virtually all of the Marriage 100 said that the first step in finding a mate is feeling good about yourself. Many mentioned how they learned to visualize the things they wanted. Try it! You'll be surprised how quickly positive thinking and, more importantly, positive *feeling and knowing*, can become a habit. If this doesn't come naturally, check out the self-help sections of your local library or bookstores—there are lots of books on visualization techniques and other ways of working on self-esteem and going after what you want. Myself, I get a lot of inspiration from books and tapes by motivational speakers such as Dr. Wayne Dyer, Marianne Williamson, and Tony Robbins.

These 100 women, in their own words and through their own personal stories, will express their opinions and attitudes on the so-called age issues and help guide you through some of the problems inherent in trying to meet the right man, dating, and, finally, saying "I do." And they won't leave you at the altar. They'll point out some of the things to expect during the sometimes difficult first year, and how to get through problems that can cloud many a marriage, including dealing with stepchildren, different attitudes toward money, and ex-wives.

Let's begin with the first of many pep talks and tips that the Marriage 100 offer throughout the book to help lift your spirits and give you hope. If you sometimes feel like a dinosaur stuck in the La Brea tar pits of negative statistics, misinformation, and the endless refrains of "You're over the hill," read on.

Listen Up

If there's one expression that helps sum up the enthusiasm these women feel for over-40 marriages, it's those three little words, "Go for it!" They turned up again and again in the survey and in conversations. Others, who didn't use those exact words, echoed similar sentiments, such as, "Go after what you want," "Don't be afraid," "Don't let anything stop you." But before you can "Go for it," you first have to meet the right man, then you have to deal with the panic attacks at the thought of changing your life to accommodate another person. And if you have a history of unhappy relationships, you want to be certain you're not putting your head in the meat grinder again.

Here are some other insights gleaned from the Marriage 100 to help start you on your path:

Age does not matter. "What matters is your attitude about yourself. If you believe that finding a good man is difficult beyond a certain age, then that belief will become a self-fulfilling prophecy," said Christine, who wed for the first time at 40. Suzanne, who wed for the second time at 50, said, "With today's medicine, 40 is not old, neither is 50."

Thumb your nose at statistics. "Statistics are only as good as they are applied," said Fay, who wed for the first time at 41. "You're an individual—not a number. Create your own odds, and get on with it."

Empower yourself. To slosh your way through the muck without getting stuck, you must have confidence in yourself. Gerry, a secretary who wed for the second time at 45, warns women to be very wary of what the media spews out: "I don't watch TV or read newspapers. I only read books that will empower me. If it makes me feel good, I continue to read it. If not, I drop it." For those of us who *do* watch TV and read newspapers, here's some advice from Nancy, who wed for the second time at 54: "When I get negative input from the media or anyone else, I turn it around by silently affirming, 'There's not a word of truth in it for me,' or 'That may be true for that person, but it's not true for me.' This doesn't mean you have to turn into an ostrich or ignore warnings, it just means you don't have to walk around accepting every negative as your own, personal truth. I found this especially helpful when I heard all that garbage about middle-aged women and their marriage prospects."

Never give up. "If Charlie was out there for me, I know there must be other good men out there for other women," said Barbara, who wed for the first time at 42. Carol, who wed for the second time at 46, said, "Even if you have to date a lot of the wrong men (as I did), eventually the right one will come along, if you don't give up."

Now that you have an idea of what these women think you should be doing or thinking or being, let's move on to Chapter 2 and find out how some of them turned their own lives around and reached that "finish line" otherwise known as the marriage altar. That finish line, of course, is really just the beginning (more on that later). For now, we'll look at how some of the Marriage 100 overcame the so-called odds and found good men to marry.

CHAPTER 2

Getting Started in the Right Direction

Marriage is not a race; you can always get there in time.

—RUSSIAN PROVERB

Do you dread family gatherings because your mother or an aunt is going to ask you—for the umpteenth time—"When are you going to marry?" "Why aren't you married yet? What's wrong?" or, "Don't you think Johnny needs a father?"

As an avid traveler, my personal favorite was, "Oh, you were in Egypt? Did you meet anyone?" If my answer was no, they'd invariably say something like, "Oh, I'm sorry" and move on to another subject, as if the sole purpose of travel for single women is to "Meet Someone." If, God forbid, you didn't run into Mr. Wonderful while you were gazing at the Pyramids, you've obviously wasted your time and money. The older you get, especially if you've never married, the more anxious they'll be for you to connect with a man so your life will have meaning. They usually mean well, of course, but they can be a royal pain. Most have probably bought into all the negative comments on the chances of a woman over 40 finding a husband.

The fact is, each year hundreds of thousands of women over 40 do "Meet Someone" and get married. So forget the negative comments and statistics and listen to the true experts: Women who've said their "I do's" in their 40s and up. They've fought the odds and reached their goals. Here's what some of them have to say about it.

EILEEN
Make sure it feels right

If you're like Eileen was before she wed Kevin, you have a successful career and a full social life, but you feel something's missing.

"I was in my 40s, never married, and my life was very full, but I wanted a partner, someone to share my life with," she said. "I used to tell myself that before I die, I would like to have a husband and experience what marriage is all about." She did, indeed, find a partner, Kevin, and they were married when she was 47 and he was 57. It was the first marriage for both of them. Actually, he had been in her life for five years before they started dating. They were both part of a large, loosely knit group that met for tennis on weekends in New York's Central Park.

"He was with another woman most of the time, so I didn't see him as anything but a casual acquaintance. We'd nod hello and that was about it," she said. "After a few months he started showing up alone and I found out his friend had died. But I still didn't think of him as someone I wanted to date. I thought he was a nice man, a pleasant person, but that was it.

"After we started dating, he told me that he had been watching me and wanted to ask me for my phone number for several weeks, but he had forgotten my name and was too embarrassed to ask."

Fate intervened, as it invariably does. One evening, as she was leaving her office near Times Square, he stepped out of a nearby coffee shop and ran into her. He swears it was a coincidence.

"He invited me for a drink, but I wanted to get home to watch an address the President was giving that evening. I invited him home to watch it with me. He did, and afterwards we went out for pizza.

"It wasn't love at first sight, but what kept going through my head that evening was, 'I've met a very nice person, a decent human being.'" They started dating steadily and were married ten months later.

Like so many single women, Eileen was loaded down with her share of negative baggage about being an "old maid," and she worried about her biological clock ticking away. Twice before, these worries got her engaged to men who weren't right for her.

"The first time I was engaged I was hitting my 30s and I felt pressure to marry because of my age," she said. "I was afraid if I didn't get a husband now, I'd never have another chance. But I got cold feet and called it off a month before the wedding. Everything was happening too fast. It just didn't feel right and I couldn't cope.

"The second time, I was in my late 30s and I was reading all those articles about my biological clock," she said. "This time, my fiance called it off and, to tell the truth, I was relieved. Both times I was extremely nervous about getting married and I guess way down deep it wasn't what I wanted, at least not with these men.

"With Kevin, my feelings were very different," she continued. "When we became engaged, I wasn't the least bit nervous, because it just felt so right. Our getting married was such a natural process that I never had any second thoughts."

Getting to that point obviously wasn't easy for Eileen. First, she had to learn to let go of the frantic search for a husband.

"I used to believe that every man who entered my life was there for one purpose—to audition for the role of being my husband," she said. "I put so much pressure on myself and my dates. Instead of simply having a good time, I was busy interviewing and observing the poor guy to see if he'd make a good husband."

Eileen said that about two years before she and Kevin got together, she gave up on her agenda of seeing every man she dated as a potential husband.

"I can thank a girlfriend for that. She suggested I start looking for friendship in a man and let go of the rest. We went through the list of all my failed relationships and she pointed out how none of the men were my friends first," she said. "It was an eye opener for me. Friendship first wasn't something I had thought about."

Another person she said she can thank is a man she once dated who wanted out of the relationship and suggested she join Al-Anon to talk about her obsessive need to get married.

"He did me a big favor, both by breaking up with me and by suggesting Al-Anon. He was a member of Alcoholics Anonymous at the time and was a big believer in Twelve-Step programs. He told me it was Al-Anon, not him, that I needed. He was right.

"Al-Anon taught me to court myself, to understand that the relationship I have with myself is the longest relationship I'll ever have," she said. "Al-Anon helped me gain self-confidence. It taught me to treat myself well because if I didn't, why should anyone else? I learned to do things alone and enjoy it. I took myself to the movies, to the beach, out to dinner. I was good to myself, so that when someone came into my life, I would know what it means to be treated well. And then, thanks to Al-Anon, I learned to let go and trust a higher power."

Eileen said she decided to keep the dream of marriage alive, but to let go of the time pressure, to just let things happen and not worry about it.

"Once I got into this process of letting go, I started enjoying life. It was great," she said. "I would say to all women who want to marry, don't let go of your dreams, just let go of the time frame. Let life unfold in its own way. You have all the time in the world."

Eileen recognizes, of course, that if you want children of your own, you don't have all the time in the world.

"You have to come to terms with that issue or else you might marry just to have children, which would be a big mistake," she continued. "I always wanted children, but as I got older I gave up on that and said, 'OK God, I will give up the kids, but not my dream of having a husband.'

"Just remember, marriage will happen to you if that's what you truly want," she said. "But it won't necessarily happen when you want it to."

And how to meet men?

"Do what you enjoy doing. Kevin's sister, a widow, met her second husband in a birdwatching club—that's what she enjoys. I met Kevin playing tennis, that's what I enjoy," she said.

"Develop confidence in yourself and project it, even if that means getting professional help. Build a life for yourself that you're content with. If that's not the case right now, then go to work on making the necessary changes. Maybe you can't change everything, but change what you can. And remember, that the one thing you can always change is your attitude," she said.

What to look for in a man?

"Look for kindness," she said. "Someone who respects others, as well as yourself, and someone who wants a relationship as much as you do. Don't be desperate. It will happen when the time is right. I tell my single friends, 'Don't worry. I was 47 when I married. If I can do it, you can do it, at any age.'"

PEGGY
Trust your cat

"I was the lone holdout—all my friends married young," said Peggy, who wed at 40. "My friends didn't care that I was single, but my family did, especially my mother. At family gatherings I got the usual, 'When are you going to get married?' You learn to ignore it after a while. I wasn't worried about getting married. I was more interested in a career and in doing what I liked with my spare time, but try to explain that to your mother."

Peggy met Ian on a commuter train that serves the suburbs of Chicago. He was a conductor and, one morning, they struck up a conversation.

"I was immediately attracted to him," she said. "Most guys I had any connection with were threatened by my brains. Ian wasn't. After I'd been riding the train a while and he got to know me, he'd finish his work and come back to talk to me. He talked to me about articles he'd read in the *Wall Street Journal* and other publications. We had wonderful, intelligent conversations. I was very impressed with his mind."

After six months of this, she decided to take the first step. "I knew some of the crew and one day I asked, 'Who is this guy? Is he single?' Their eyes lit up. Not only did they tell me that he was single, but that he lived near me and boarded the train at the same station," she said. "I gave them my phone number, which they passed along to him, but he never called. It didn't really surprise me, because I could tell he was painfully shy.

"Three months later I saw him board the train at my station and decided to take the bull by the horns. I said to him, 'We're just neighbors, why don't you give me a call sometime?' He was flabbergasted, totally speechless," she said.

Not one to give up easily, Peggy tried again a week later and asked him to have dinner with her before a party they were both planning to attend in the city. It turned out to be a very difficult first date.

"We were part of a save-the-trains group that had lobbied successfully in the state capital and we were invited to a party hosted by a state representative," said Peggy. "I suggested we have dinner together beforehand.

"It was very difficult. I almost didn't want to see him again," she continued. "He was very, very hard to talk to, answering yes or no and doing nothing to keep the conversation going, so different from our talks on the train where the conversation flowed easily. After the first half-hour, I was ready to give up. But my intuition told me to keep on, that he was worth it. I'm so glad I didn't quit."

It took her a few more dates to break the ice, but slowly and gradually Ian came out of his shell. They were married six months after their first date. She was 40, he was 43, the first time for both of them.

"My advice is persevere, and always listen to that little voice inside of you, it's always right," she said. "I felt very comfortable about marrying Ian. This was the guy, I just knew it."

Not only did Peggy trust her own instincts, but she also listened to her cat, Gracie.

"He loved Gracie and she loved him. That was very important to me because this cat is very perceptive, a really good judge of character," she said. "I had a date with a cop one time. The minute he came through the door Gracie arched up and hissed at him—all her hair stood on end. She was right to dislike him; he turned out to be your basic jerk. But when Ian walked through the door for the first time, Gracie twirled around his legs and wouldn't let him walk. The minute he sat down, she was on his lap. It was love at first sight, for both of them."

Peggy said before she met Ian she was content with her single life and wasn't particularly interested in marriage.

"I didn't necessarily want to be single for the rest of my life, but I didn't give marriage much thought, either. I was happy and involved in a number of activities," she said. "I was working full time as a loan specialist for the city, and taking writing and art courses at night. Finding a man just wasn't a priority."

Peggy believes strongly that you should develop self-reliance before you even think of marrying, a lesson she said her sister learned the hard way.

"My younger sister got married right out of high school—biggest mistake she ever made. She gave up a college scholarship to marry a man in the Navy who wanted her at his beck and call when he came home after being away at sea. I warned her, 'This is a big mistake.' I told her what I'd tell any woman at any age, 'Take care of yourself first, protect your own interests, know you can earn a living and be on your own; then, and only then, consider marriage.' She resented my advice, married him, and didn't talk to me for months. The marriage ended in divorce, needless to say, and now she admits I was right."

Like Eileen, Peggy stresses the importance of looking for friendship in a man first, rather than expecting instant romance.

"If you don't have a friendship, you're in trouble," she said. "A husband who's also a friend is someone you can depend on for the rest of your life," she said. "And don't give up being yourself just because you have found a man. So many women I know focus on being taken care of, rather than on taking care of themselves. They know nothing about finances, credit, mortgages—what a mistake!"

Her bottom line: "Be your own person, have lots of interests, and always listen to your cat."

EMILY

Just leave it alone

"Stop looking and it'll happen all by itself. The harder you work at finding a husband, the more likely it is you'll find the wrong person, that you'll settle for less than you deserve because you're too anxious. Just leave it alone and it'll happen."

That's Emily's advice and she should know, for her marriage to David was the third time around for both of them. She was 45, he was 63 when they wed. She has two grown children, he has four, and between the two of them there are six grandchildren. Emily said that when she met David, getting involved with a man again was the last thing on her mind.

"I think dating sucks," she said. "When I met David I hadn't dated for ages, because I found it very difficult, especially when you've been out of it for a while. I didn't want another man in my life. I was burned out." She met David on a blind date set up by mutual friends. We'll hear more about that in Chapter 5.

Like so many of the Marriage 100, Emily cautions women to be certain they're marrying for the right reasons. She has this advice for any woman, of any age, contemplating marriage:

"First of all, if you're marrying for love, be sure it really *is* love that you feel, that it's not just lust or fear of being alone.

"Second, be certain you can live well on your own before you try to find a husband—don't expect a man to make up what's missing in your life. It never works. Trust me, I've been there, I know.

"Third, be comfortable in your own body, stand on your own two feet, and be yourself. That's the only way you'll attract a man who's right for you."

For Emily, the right man is an older man, and she sings the praises of older men, "My husband is eighteen years older than I am. I can't talk to younger men—they're idiots, so limited in their conversational skills. I was married to a man my own age for twenty years. He was an idiot from day one and it never got better. As for men younger than myself, I have one word, 'Yuck!' I can appreciate the sex appeal of a younger man, but I prefer a man whose life is etched on his face. I fell into David's eyes the moment we met and saw his whole life in those eyes."

SUZANNE

Be what you want to attract

Suzanne is a big believer in that old saying, "You attract what you are."

"I was single and living alone for seventeen years when I met Tommy," said Suzanne, a stock broker who wed for the second time at 45. They met at a dinner in Los Angeles honoring a local art society.

"Until you have matured and grown into the kind of person you would like *him* to be, you won't attract the right person for you or appreciate him even if you do meet him," she said. "*Be* what you want to attract. You want kindness, generosity? Then be kind and generous yourself. If you have an ideal of what you want in a man, see how close to that ideal you are yourself. If you're not, start working on yourself. Develop the traits you admire in others."

For her, important traits to look for in a man include integrity, high self-esteem, emotional stability, and a sense of humor.

"If I had to pick one trait, it would be integrity. My first husband had no integrity—he was a womanizer who lied to me all the time," she said. "I was 23 when I married him. At that time what I wanted in a man were good looks, sexiness, and the potential for a high income. And that's exactly what I got, along with a lot of unhappiness I didn't bargain for. The marriage lasted five years.

"By the time Tommy came into my life, I had a good income of my own, so I didn't care about a man's income, I didn't care whether a man was handsome, and I knew that sexiness was in the eye of the beholder," she continued. "What I wanted was a man of integrity and a man who would be faithful to me. With Tommy, I got it all—looks, sexiness, money, *and* integrity. I can't believe my good fortune. It's not dumb luck; the truth is, I care a lot about integrity. I live my life with honesty and integrity, and so do my close friends. That was a priority for me, and that's the quality in Tommy that I fell in love with.

"The bottom line is, if you don't like the type of men you've attracted in the past, then concentrate on being what you want to attract."

Karen
Keep the door open

"Go out as much as you can and keep the door open. You never can tell who's going to walk into your life."

That's Karen, a widow in her 60s who married a man she met at her first husband's funeral. Jack, her current husband, was her first husband's college classmate and the two men stayed in touch over the years. Karen knew of him but they never met—until the funeral.

"Jack was a widower by then and I think he had his eye on me at the funeral, but I didn't notice him at first because I was too distraught," she said.

"Before my first husband's death, I assumed that if I were alone, my chances of remarrying were slim. My first husband was very keen on my remarrying. I always told him that *he* was in the seller's market, not me, because there are five widows to each widower. I told him he could remarry in a minute but it wouldn't be so easy for me. But there you have it, I met one husband at the other husband's funeral." She was 67 and Jack was 72 when they wed.

While she doesn't recommend hanging out at funeral parlors, she does recommend staying busy and in circulation, regardless of age and circumstances.

"My story just goes to show how you never know when or how someone is going to enter your life," she said. "Explore life as much as you can. Stay in circulation, whether that means going to church, joining a theater club, a health club, or simply going out with your women friends. The important thing is to get out of the house and start circulating. I can't think of any other way to meet men. Basically it's just luck, but you increase your chances of finding a mate by staying active and meeting many different types of people. It also makes your life much more interesting."

She also said, "Don't be too critical of others. You're not perfect and neither is anybody else. And what's more, don't think you're going to change anybody because, after a certain age, people are more or less set in their ways."

Karen said one of the really nice things about an older marriage is the shift in priorities, from always thinking about the future, to living in the now.

"When I was much younger, I was very ambitious. I wanted a man who would make it Big Time—and I got that in my first husband, who was very successful," she said. "Now that kind of thing no longer matters, since 'The paths of glory lead but to the grave.'

"In this marriage, our energy level ain't what it used to be, but our capacity for living intensely in the present is better than ever."

LOIS

Don't let 'em get you down

"I'm a reject from a dating service," said Lois, who wed for the first time at 44. "If I could overcome that blow to my self-esteem and go on to marry a wonderful man, anyone can.

"What happened was, I went to a video dating service in Los Angeles feeling really miserable after just ending a two-year relationship. The relationship was never a good one. In fact, from the very beginning it was a totally disastrous, self-defeating thing," she said. "After we broke up, I started searching for ways to meet new men. First, I joined a couple of women's groups in an effort to get over my depression and regain my sense of self-worth, but they were no help whatsoever. All I heard was how terrible men are, and how California men are especially bad. One of the groups, called 'Breakups,' was all about how relationships never last—either they end in death or the man walks out on you. Really uplifting stuff."

Now, more depressed than ever, she went to a video dating service, which turned out to be an even greater disaster.

"I couldn't believe it! They refused to accept me! Have you ever heard of anyone being rejected by a dating service? They said that by talking to me and looking at me in the teleprompter and watching my body language, it was obvious that I was miserable and unhappy. They said I was wasting my money—nobody would be interested in me.

"I wasn't aware I was projecting so much negativity," she said. "I can laugh about it now, but I was devastated at the time."

Family and neighbors didn't help much either.

"A neighbor of mine, a man, used to constantly ask, 'How come you're not married?' One day I said, 'Is it bothering you?' He left me alone after that.

"And then there was my mother," she continued. "Mom was concerned that she had two unmarried daughters on her hands, both over 30. Even when my sister and I were in our 20s, she was concerned about our still being single. I was about 24 and my sister, 21, when mom related a very catty remark a friend of hers had made about our being 'spinsters.' It really embarrassed her that we were unmarried, even then. When my sister married at 38, mom sort of relaxed about my being single and finally left me alone on the subject. I guess she was relieved that she had been able to marry off at least one of her daughters."

Lois said that after the video dating fiasco, she gave up the search and buried herself in her work as a book editor, and spent all of her spare time hiking with the Sierra Club.

"I was burned out. I hiked with the club in Griffith Park every night after work and every weekend," she said. "I did it for my mental, emotional, and physical well-being." And that's how she met Charles, a fellow hiking addict.

"Before I got to know Charles, I went out with some of the men I met hiking, but they always turned out to be jerks," she said. "There was always something wrong with them. For one thing they were cheap—oh, my Lord, were they cheap! It was as if they were using the hikes for free dates. I didn't find anyone I wanted to date, and after a while I just didn't care.

"The hiking kept me busy. I guess you could say I felt a certain amount of loneliness during that period, but I also felt more peaceful than I had in several years," she continued. "I decided that this was how my life was shaping up, and I was reasonably content with it. I wasn't pushing for anything anymore."

Lois had been hiking with the club for about a year when she met Charles. At first, both were more interested in hiking than in each other.

"We're both very quiet types, but eventually we started chatting as we hiked and I really began to like him," she said. "What I first liked about him was that he is a true gentleman—very polite and considerate of others."

After one of the hikes, he invited her out for pizza. They were married two years and many hikes later—and they're still hiking those hills above Hollywood.

"If you're out searching all the time, you probably won't meet anybody," she said. "When I met Charles, I didn't care about meeting men, I was just going along with my life. I think once you relax and stop searching, it's easier for someone to come into your life."

BARBARA
Nothing's wrong with you

Barbara was 42 and a New York public relations executive when she wed for the first time—but not before a tremendous amount of soul-searching.

"By the time I hit 40, I was extremely depressed. I wondered, 'What's wrong with me?' There was so much negative publicity about being over 35 and *still* single. Those horrible articles about our marriage chances getting slimmer, and our biological clocks ticking away confirmed all of my worse fears—that time had run out, that my chances of connecting with someone were virtually nil, and that I'd never have children of my own," she said. "It drove me straight into therapy.

"My therapist pooh-poohed it all," she continued. "He said that there are plenty of older women out there connecting with good men. But I didn't buy it. I knew the prospects were not good and that they were not going to get better, at least not for me."

Her mother and sister made matters worse by harping on her unmarried status and, worse yet, by feeling sorry for her.

"My younger sister, who is married with three kids, would look at me with tears in her eyes. She would say things such as, 'You of all people. You're so giving. There should be somebody out there for you.' My mother would nod her head in agreement. Between the two of them, I felt like a failure. When I told them I was finally getting married, they were amazed and delighted, but they still had to add that they couldn't understand why it hadn't happened sooner," she said.

Why didn't she marry earlier?

"Marriage, per se, wasn't all that important to me. It still isn't. What was important was to find someone I could connect with on a visceral level, and for a long time," she said. "I wanted a partner, a counterpart. Forever is great, but forever is not always forever."

With the help of her therapist, she began to focus on all the things she liked about her life.

"Slowly I began to shift my focus away from what I didn't have and toward all the good things in my life. Then I lost two very dear friends to AIDS. In a sad and ironic way, it was through my deep sense of loss that I began to really appreciate my friends and the loving relationships that were all around me," she said.

Barbara believes strongly that once she made that fundamental shift in outlook, from seeing the cup half empty to seeing it half full, she was ready to meet the man who would become her husband.

"What worked for me was to get reconciled to what I had at the time, rather than always focusing on what I didn't have. As soon as I managed to do that, Charlie showed up. Now I don't know if it's that clear a cause and effect, but I do know that if Charlie had come along earlier, I probably wouldn't have noticed him because he's quiet and shy and not at all what I used to think was my type," she said. "It just seems that when I became comfortable with myself and the life I had created for myself, I was open to meeting a person like Charlie."

Barbara said a major prejudice she had to overcome before she met Charlie was taking a second look at men over 35 who had never married. Charlie, like herself, was 40 when they met and single all his life.

"For years I refused to date men who had never married," she continued. "I was certain there had to be something wrong with them. I thought if a man was still single at 35, he was single for a reason—no one would have him. But my need to connect made me set aside this particular prejudice, just this one time. Thank God I did."

She met Charlie, a college professor, through Single Booklovers, a national organization that encourages people to get acquainted through correspondence before meeting face to face. We'll hear more about that in Chapter 6.

VIVIAN

Make a list

"After two failed marriages and two long, but failed relationships, I was sick of men," said Vivian, a factory worker who eventually overcame that feeling and wed for the third time at 42. "Until I met Ray I always picked men who were wrong for me. I didn't think there was anyone out there who wanted the same things I did and who shared some of the same feelings."

Vivian said she had a watershed experience when a three-year affair ended and she realized that man was just like her two previous husbands.

"It was like a bulb going off in my head," she said. "Finally, I realized that I was attracted to a certain type of man and that this type was totally wrong for me."

Vivian realized she had to give serious thought to what she really wanted in a man and to set some priorities. She went to work on herself and a few months later met Ray. But it didn't happen without a lot of soul-searching and, perhaps, a little bit of divine intervention.

"I made a list of fifteen characteristics I wanted in a man and I swore I would never get involved with someone who didn't have those qualities," she said. "After I completed the list, I put it in my Bible and prayed for guidance. After that, I felt at peace with myself for the first time in years. I forgot about the list and went on with my life. Four months later I met Ray. I remembered the list, pulled it out, and saw that he passed with flying colors. He still does, after seven years of a very happy marriage."

Here are some of the qualities she included in her list:

- Someone who can accept me as I am and not try to change me into someone I can't be.
- Someone who cares about what I feel.
- Someone who will pick up after himself.

"Ask yourself, 'What's important to me?' Then make a list and tuck it away for future reference," said Vivian. "When you make a list, you clarify what want, you learn to focus—it goes a long way in helping you know when the right man for you comes along. And it doesn't hurt to pray a lot."

GERRY

Honor yourself

"Work on your own self-esteem. When you honor and love yourself, the right person will come along that will also honor and love you."

Gerry, a secretary, who wed for the second time at 45, said it took her a long time to learn that lesson.

"After my divorce, I stayed single for ten years," she said. "I didn't have kids and I lived alone. I also didn't have a lot of friends, didn't date much, and had very little money to spend, so I didn't go out much. I was lonely, but happier than I had been during my first marriage.

"I dated a guy from work once in a while, but it wasn't serious. My major entertainment was belonging to a church choir, something I genuinely loved," she continued.

Gerry said she gained a lot of insights into herself through adult education classes in self-awareness at a local college. These helped her learn to be at peace with herself.

"I went to a therapist once, but I didn't go back because I knew there was nothing wrong with me," she said. "Instead, I enrolled in classes and hit the books. There are lots of classes on various self-help teachings. I took one on Transactional Analysis, for example, that was very helpful. Adult education classes are an inexpensive way to expand your horizons or go inward to better understanding of yourself and the world around you.

"You can also find lots of self-help books in the public library. Start taking classes, start reading, and you'll find a whole new world opening up to you, with new, caring people entering your life."

Gerry said that since so many of our beliefs on marriage come from our parents, who themselves may have been unhappy, you tend to repeat their mistakes.

"Because no one instructs us in marriage, we usually bring our mother's beliefs into our marriages, and her beliefs came from her mother, and on and on. If those beliefs didn't work for our mothers, they're probably not going to work for us," she said. "My mother, for example, controlled my father and so it follows that I controlled my first husband. To break the pattern, you have to be conscious of it in the first place."

Gerry first got acquainted with her future husband, Mike, through work—but only on the telephone.

"He would call to speak to my boss, and if he wasn't immediately available, Mike and I would chat a while. Eventually I gave him my home number," she said. "We talked on the phone for three months before we actually met, despite the fact he only lived seven minutes away. I think we were afraid of meeting face to face. We both had been burned in our first marriages and had a fear of relationships. I think we also felt, 'This is really working over the phone, so why spoil it?'"

When they finally got up the nerve to meet, he rode over to her house on a bike.

"My first impression was, 'He's so short!' He's 5'2" and I'm 5' 10". But even though he was short, I knew he was special. I felt right away, this was going to work."

They were engaged in three weeks and married six months later, both for the second time. She didn't have children, but he made up for it with three grown children and five grandchildren.

"I think the greatest reward in being married is having a supportive spouse," she said. "The greatest challenge is to leave the lines of communication open and clear. I think this is a special problem for women. Sometimes we go the old way of being, hoping men know what we want, or yelling at them if they don't come through for us. We need to clearly ask for what we want and see that it gets done—this is not always easy for women over 40 who've been raised to get what they want through indirect means. I know it's something I had to learn to do."

One example she gives is letting her husband know that she needs to be alone every morning to meditate.

"I told Mike that I need my own space in the morning—I go into my study for an hour and he doesn't disturb me," she said. "That didn't happen automatically, I had to tell him."

Today, Gerry is a published author of self-help books and a popular speaker on metaphysics in adult education classes at high schools throughout New Jersey.

"During my first marriage I had been a member of a Christian fundamentalist church. When I left my husband, my friends shunned me because they think divorce is a sin," she said. "I then turned to other, less conservative Christian churches, but it just didn't work for me. A woman at work introduced me to metaphysics and I started going to Unity services in New York. I also read everything I could get my hands on concerning higher consciousness and our link with the universe. It turned my life around—those ten years between marriages were my greatest growth period."

One of the things she always emphasizes in her talks is, "You need to support people at their highest levels. When you do, you will attract people who will do the same for you."

DOTTIE

Resolve differences first

It's not always "happily ever after." Some of the Marriage 100, such as Dottie, are having serious problems. She's a stockbroker who wed for the first time at 41. In Dottie's case, her marriage is rocky because her husband, Burt, wants children and she doesn't, and each thought the other would have a change of heart after they were married. Dottie has learned the hard way that people don't change after they're married.

"We lived together for two years before we were married and during that time he talked a lot about having children," she said. "I told him I didn't want children, but I wasn't as firm about it as I should have been and I wasn't paying attention to how much it meant to him. I guess we both hoped the other would have a change of heart after we were married, but so far, neither of us has.

"We still haven't worked it out and we both regret not having settled the issue before we wed," she continued. "This is a problem that may break up our marriage.

"My mother left when I was very young. I have no maternal memory and don't know much about mothering," she said. "I guess Frank thought that through the stability of our marriage, I'd change my mind and feel more secure about my ability to be a good mother. Although I haven't closed the door on it yet, I still don't think I want children and I know I'd better decide soon because I'm not getting any younger. Adoption is not an option. I'm open to it, but he's not.

"You can't change someone after marriage," she continued. "If he tells you he wants children or doesn't want children, listen to him—he means it. And make sure he listens to you, too."

Still, they continue to talk about it, trying to work it out. It's made Dottie a big believer in the importance of good communication between couples.

"Communication is a major skill," she said. "If you don't communicate, your problems get worse. There's usually not enough talking in a relationship. And not enough listening."

Terry
Don't get desperate

Terry, who wed for the second time at 41, believes that women, like men and good wine, get better with age.

"You don't know what's going on or get your act together until you're about 50, then you finally start to understand what you're all about," she said. "Don't get desperate. Know that you don't need to marry to be happy and fulfilled."

Terry was a real estate broker and single mother of three when mutual friends introduced her to Ed, a retired Army officer. Ironically, Terry and Ed lived three doors apart in the same condo complex but had never seen each other.

"My ex-husband was also in the military. A couple of his old friends called me one day to say they'd be in town and would like to see me. When I invited them to dinner and gave them directions to my apartment, they said, 'We were just there last night.' It turns out Ed had invited them to his place the night before. They were convinced that this was too much of a coincidence for it not to be fate. They tried to fix me up with him, but I told them, 'No, I'm busy with work and my children, I have no intention of dating again.'"

She gave in when they insisted she meet them at their hotel for just a quick glass of wine.

"I said, 'OK, a fifteen-minute glass of wine. That's it.' But, of course, fifteen minutes turned into a long evening with the four of us going out to dinner together," she said. "Because of our military backgrounds, we found we had many friends in common and we swapped lots of funny stories from our military days. I found Ed charming and witty."

The following evening Terry and Ed had dinner together with friends of his.

"I'll never forget it. I was dressed to the nines in a designer pants suit. We were in the bar of an elegant restaurant waiting for a table, sitting on bar stools laughing. At one point I couldn't stop laughing—I leaned back and fell over backwards, my feet in the air. And I hadn't even been drinking. I'm a former model, very stately and sophisticated looking—this was the last thing you'd expect from me. Instead of head over heels, I fell heels over head, and I was mortified," she said, adding that she survived and they were married a year and a half later.

SALLY
Develop your self-esteem

Not all the women in the survey were self-confident and independent types. Sally, a widow who wed for the second time at 57, didn't develop self-esteem until she was in her early 50s.

"I didn't attract men when I was young. I wasn't pretty. I was shy, withdrawn, and very thin with round shoulders," she said. "Then I got self-esteem. Several people asked me what happened, and said, 'Whatever it was, it's good.' I married at 47 for the first time, and 57 the second time, and I attracted lots of men while I was between marriages."

How did she develop self-esteem?

"I learned to concentrate on my good qualities and be more outgoing," she said. "Then I met my first husband and he helped me by complimenting me a lot. At first I didn't believe him, but then I thought, 'Hey, he's right.' My second husband, Bernie, never compliments me. At first I was angry, but it made me grow up because it helped me realize that I don't have to be dependent on someone else's opinion of me to be happy. That, too, has given me confidence."

Sally met her second husband five years before her first husband died. After she was widowed, she remembered an incident three years before that prompted her to look up Bernie.

"He was helping us with a car that was having problems. He lifted the car. I'll never forget that," she said. "I admired his strength. I still do."

So, what's a person to do? As you can see, these women have many different takes on how to get started in the right direction. Below are more ideas. Pick the ones that feel right for you and try them out. What have you got to lose?

Listen Up

Some say, "Let go, stop looking"; others, "Never give up, even if you have to date a lot of the wrong men." And yet others say, "Always be open to new experiences, go out a lot, make an effort to meet new people." The laid back (or burned out) ones say, "Relax, don't worry about it, do what interests you, that's how you'll find someone who's right for you."

Confused? Don't be. When it comes to attitudes or game plans, it's obvious that one size does not fit all. But there is one thing virtually all of the women agreed upon—the importance of creating an interesting, active lifestyle for yourself that you genuinely enjoy, with or without a man. As one woman said, "Women who are financially and psychologically independent have the luxury of marrying for love, not need." So, stay busy, stay interesting, stay out there, and read on.

Say yes. "If marriage is what you want, say yes and go for it," said Renee, who wed for the second time at 48. But how do you "Go for it"? Renee advises saying yes to friends who say, "I've got a great guy for you," saying yes to social invitations you might otherwise turn down, and to exploring travel, adult education, or anything else that sparks your interest. Billie, who wed for the second time at 48, said, "I have always believed that if a woman is truly interested in meeting an eligible man, she will. It's a function of openness and willingness to commit."

Kiss the frogs good-bye. "You may have to kiss 100 frogs before you find your prince, but it's worth it," said Jane, a first-time bride at 47. And if the reverse happens, if your prince turns into a frog? "Say good-bye and move on." Susan, who wed for the third time at 40, added, "If I could say one thing to women, it would be, 'Wait for the best for you, it will come. Don't settle for less.'"

Be happy with yourself. Nobody can make you happy, only you can do that. If you try to find happiness through another person, you're bound to fail. At least half the women made comments to that effect, and the ones who felt most emphatic about it were those who had married young expecting marriage and a husband to totally fulfill them. "Be happy and like yourself," said Denise, who married for the third time at 59. "Until you do that, you will not attract the right man. I married for the first time at 19 and the second time at 37. Both marriages ended in divorce. I was looking for peace and happiness outside myself, a big mistake." Bobbie, who wed for the first time at 42, said, "It's important to feel comfortable with yourself before you try to find a husband. When you're comfortable with yourself, people are comfortable with you." And Merriam, who wed for the third time at 56, said, "Women today have so many more choices, we're very lucky. We can live a full life, either single or married, alone or as a couple—take your pick."

Get active. "Get active physically and get busy doing things that excite you." That's the advice of Liz, who wed for the second time at 40. "Age? I don't let that stuff bother me. I'm too active and too busy," said Julie, who wed for the second time at 42. "Remember, the more active you are physically, the better you feel, and the better you look."

Get real. "It seems to me that so many ordinary women have the expectation of being swept away by a wealthy, globe-trotting, dashing, romantic man, completely unencumbered of responsibilities," said Ella, a math teacher who wed for the second time at 57. "Get rid of those girlhood fantasies. You'd be surprised how many nice men are out there who may not be wealthy or movie-star handsome, but who would make terrific husbands."

Know what you want. "Know what you want in a husband and when you get involved with someone, let him know who you are and what you want," said Beth, who wed for the second time at 50. Ruth, who wed for the third time at 56, added, "Do not keep going with Mr. Wrong. If he's not what you want in a husband, break up with him and keep looking—Mr. Right is out there." Like so many of the others, she, too, is a big believer in being upfront: "Be as honest as possible, first with yourself, and then with men you date. Don't have any pretenses, it's the only way you'll attract someone who loves you for yourself."

Be self-sufficient. "It's vital that you know you can support yourself, travel, have fun, without a man, so that when you do marry, you'll enter the relationship from strength, not weakness," said Jane, who wed for the first time at 47. Anne, who wed for the second time at 40, said, "Before I met my current husband, I was very happy with my life. My divorce from my first husband was very painful, but a tremendous learning experience. It taught me to be self-sufficient and to be very comfortable with who I am." Candice, who met her husband on a ski slope, added, "If you want to meet a great guy, go to the top of the mountain and be proficient. Any guy who's worth his salt isn't going to fall for that helpless stuff."

Forget the past. "It's important to put the past and its failures and disappointments behind you," said Arlene, who wed for the second time at 52. "If you concentrate on the past, you're likely to attract the same types and repeat the mistakes. Look forward, not backward."

These are just a few of the many ideas and anecdotes the Marriage 100 will be sharing with you throughout this book.

In the next chapter, we'll look at the questionnaire itself and how the women answered specific questions—questions that, perhaps, are very much on your mind. And, hopefully, the answers to those questions will help you move forward on your own path.

CHAPTER 3

The Heart of the Matter

May the single be married and the married happy.
—AMERICAN PROVERB

In putting together the questionnaire, I imagined myself sitting with women friends around a large table in someone's dining room, in a warm, relaxed atmosphere. With a steaming coffee mug in one hand, a pencil in the other, and a yellow legal pad in front of me, I'm busy asking questions and jotting down advice and information as it bounces around the table from one woman to another.

In this chapter, we'll sit around that table together and see what some of the Marriage 100 have to say on a variety of issues, from how to find the right man and whether there's such a thing as love at first sight, to matters such as how much "togetherness" couples really need, and the importance of sex, religion, and mutual interests, not necessarily in that order. I picked eight open-ended questions from the questionnaire that I believe get to the heart of the matter, questions that sparked the most interest and generated the greatest variety of answers, both in the written form and during the telephone interviews.

There are no right or wrong answers to any of these questions—the women all speak from their own experiences and, hopefully, some of their answers will resonate with you and help you along in your own quest to find and marry a good man.

Not all of their stories have happy endings. Two of the women participated in the survey despite the fact that their latest marriage was failing. They wanted to talk about what went wrong in the hope that others might learn from their mistakes. So picture yourself at that table, sit back, relax, and listen up.

Question: What advice would you give women over 40 who would like to marry or remarry?

My own advice would be, do your own thing, but always have your antennae out, and be open and receptive to meeting new types of men. Don't limit yourself to what you wanted when you were in your 20s or 30s. At that age you were probably looking for an ideal that most likely never existed, anyway. Let's see what others have to say on the subject.

CAROLINE
Get a life

Caroline, a grade school teacher, divorced her first husband when she was 37, after a fifteen-year marriage and four children, ranging in age from 10 to 14. At age 58 she married Robert, a lawyer, whom she met through his daughter, a fellow teacher.

When asked if she was actively looking for a husband or a long-term relationship, her answer was, "Not specifically. After my divorce, I dated a bit, and then had a long affair. When that ended, I felt that was probably it, as far as men were concerned. I decided to devote myself to my work and my friends."

Caroline was a traditional, stay-at-home mom during most of her first marriage and returned to teaching part-time about two years before her divorce. Most of the time she lived through her family. After her divorce she went straight into a relationship that took up most of her time and energy. It wasn't until that relationship ended that she realized she needed to get a life.

"I was in my 40s when I came to the conclusion that I had to have a career I loved, friends, hobbies—a life of my own, no matter what. And I had to be good to myself," she said. "While it's important to get out there and try to meet men, it's a mistake to focus on trying to meet 'Mr. Right'—focus on what's the best life you can make for yourself, with or without a man."

JO
Know what you want

Jo, also a teacher and divorcee, remarried at age 48. She met her second husband, Andrew, an art dealer, when she answered a personal ad he had placed in a city lifestyle magazine. Her mantra is clarity. You need clarity to find the right man, or to achieve anything else you want in life.

"Be clear about the lifestyle and kind of person you want," she said. "Some of the best advice I ever got on meeting men was through a seminar I attended called, 'How To Have the Relationship You Want Without Efforting.'

"First, we focused on exactly what kind of relationship we wanted—do you really want marriage or do you, in fact, want lots of dates? Many women think they want marriage, but when push comes to shove, they often find that they don't want that much of a commitment. Then we worked on being clear on what type of lifestyle we *really* wanted," she said. "Sometimes you think you want one thing, when in fact, down deep, you want the opposite.

"I knew I wanted marriage. But then I had to ask myself, 'What are the traits I want in a man?' I gave it a lot of thought and made lists of what I wanted," she continued. "*The* most important thing that I learned from the seminar and that I took to heart was this: *the person I want to be with must want to be with me.* This may sound obvious, but it's not. Many single people spend months or years with someone who, indeed, has all the right qualities for them, but who does not want to be with them on a permanent basis, or who does not want the same kind of relationship. They think they're going to change them—sometimes they do, but usually they don't. It doesn't matter what wonderful traits a man has, if you want to get married and he does not, or if he has everything you want and he seems interested in somebody else, forget him.

"The other thing I learned was, *you will know in three weeks if this man is the marrying kind*. This doesn't mean that you're going to be engaged in three weeks, it simply means that you will know if the person you've just started to date is a good prospect. If he is not, drop him—keep him as a friend, if you want, but certainly not as a potential husband. You're wasting your time."

Jo also stressed, "Be very clear on how you want to live. If you like apartment living and city life, and he yearns for a quiet life in the country, or vice versa, you are not going to have a happy relationship, let alone a lasting marriage.

"Also very important is accepting the status quo. A man is not going to change," she continued. "If you don't like what you see, find someone else. That doesn't mean you can't make compromises. You can, and will, make lots of compromises, but only if you know this is a man who *wants* to be with you and who shares your same basic lifestyle and interests. Then, and only then, can you accept something that isn't so perfect."

Jo said that once you do get involved with someone who seems right for you, it's important to focus on his positive traits and accept things you don't like about him.

"In my case I've had to deal with a husband who rarely tells me upfront if something is bugging him," she said. "If Andrew's angry at me, he doesn't come out and say so, he just makes things difficult for me in a thousand small ways. I went to a therapist for help and I learned to deal with it, mostly by simply walking out of the room when he starts carrying on. Putting up with his passive-aggressive behavior is a compromise I've made, but it's OK because he has other qualities that are wonderful."

MOLLY

Don't be pressured into marriage

Molly, an attorney who wed for the second time at 42, is another one who urges that you be clear on the reason you are marrying. Her two-year-old marriage to a psychotherapist is failing and she blames herself for not paying attention to her inner voice, which was screaming, "Don't marry him!"

"You must be clear about why you want to marry, in general, and why you want to marry this person, in particular," she said. "Looking back, I realized I married the wrong man and for all the wrong reasons, and this marriage is ending," she said. "If I had it to do over again, I would just live with a man. I married mainly because he wanted to. Then I started selling the idea of marriage to myself, even though everything inside me shouted, 'No!' I had been single for eleven years and I told myself that it was time for me to settle down, have a home, etc. But that's not a reason to marry, under any circumstances, and it certainly was not what I really wanted out of life.

"I was 19 when I married for the first time (but eight or so emotionally). It lasted fifteen years and we have three children. After my divorce, I worked my way through college and law school—and just when I was finally independent, emotionally and financially, I married again. Unfortunately, I chose a similar personality type in both husbands, not quite so pronounced in the second, but still there. Both were alcoholics, like my father, both were abusive, like my father."

While Molly is not against marriage, she does think it's important that women marry out of strength, not weakness.

"We don't have to have a man to validate us as we get older. If we do, we are in deep trouble," she said. "If we think a man is necessary to complete us as human beings, we need to reassess our mental programs."

ANNETTE
Find by not looking

Annette, a novelist and college teacher, married for the first time at 44. She met her husband, Marv, when she took a secretarial job at his construction firm.

"The best way to look for men is not to look," she said. "I never thought about marriage. I did things that interested me, I never did things because I might meet a man. Enjoy your life day-to-day and *if* you find someone to share it with, fine. If not, it won't matter that much because you'll have a fulfilling life anyway."

Annette also believes in taking the lead when it comes to meeting new people and making new friends, of either sex.

"Bring people into your life; don't wait for them to include you in theirs," she said. "And if you yearn for children, get involved with your nieces and nephews, or children of your friends. That's what I did. That way you can enjoy the fun of taking kids on outings and indulging them for an afternoon or a weekend, but you don't have to put up with their temper tantrums or all the other things they do that annoy their parents."

FRAN
Don't panic

Another who believes you find by not looking is Fran, a writer and artist who wed for the second time at 45 after being single for thirteen years.

"If you worry too much about meeting men, it becomes a panic thing, and the chances are it won't happen," she said. "I've always found that good things tend to happen when your focus is elsewhere. If you dread the thought of remaining single, you come across as desperate. People can smell it. It's important to relax and just get comfortable with yourself.

"I have a friend who wanted to get married so-o-o bad men would turn and run after the first or second date. Around the time it became cool not to be married, she started to relax about it. I lost track of her, so I don't know whether she eventually married. But I do know that once she loosened up about it, she was a lot more fun to be around," she said.

Fran is a big believer in the Twelve-Step programs, not only for working out problems, but for meeting people who are supportive of your efforts to set goals and reach them.

"Most large cities have hundreds of Twelve-Step programs, not just for substance abusers, such as Alcoholic Anonymous or Narcotics Anonymous, but for lots of different interests," she said. "For example, Arts Anonymous, which I belonged to for several years, is a wonderful organization for people who have artistic aspirations but who are having trouble working up the guts to do what they want to do."

She first became involved in a Twelve-Step program when she joined Al-Anon to help her get out of a relationship she had with a man addicted to cocaine.

"They gave me the courage to break up with him," she continued. "Then, through Al-Anon, I heard about Arts Anonymous.

"I can't recommend these programs highly enough. They're especially helpful if you're locked into a relationship or lifestyle you don't like. Joining one is a very proactive thing to do. You'll make new friends and find people to do things with, and that's very important, whether or not you meet your future husband."

Nancy

Don't look hungry

Another who warns about being too eager is Nancy, an accountant in Colorado Springs who wed for the second time at 54. She met her husband, Tom, an attorney, on a group hike through the foothills of the Rockies. Like Annette, she was doing what she liked to do and wasn't looking for a relationship. In her case, she wasn't looking because she didn't like male attitudes toward single women, especially toward mature, single women.

"I decided I would rather be alone than put up with men who thought they were doing me a favor by inviting me to dinner," she said. "I think sometimes women are too hungry for male companionship and come across as desperately searching for a mate. That's a big mistake because that's when you end up with someone who's just interested in sex or who is insensitive to your needs.

"Don't rush into a relationship if it doesn't feel right to you—stay cool, eventually the right one for you will come along and he'll be worth waiting for."

Virginia

Forget age

For Virginia, who was 41 when she married for the first time, age is not an issue.

"Age does not matter, what matters is your attitude about yourself—if you believe meeting a man is difficult beyond a certain age, it will be," she said.

CARLA
Set goals and be specific

Carla, a retired saleswoman who was widowed once and divorced once, married for the third time at age 60. She met Bill, a marketing executive, at a friend's party in Los Angeles. Like Jo, she also enrolled in a workshop designed to help her reach her goals, which included marrying again.

"The workshop was in July and my goal was to bring a special man into my life," she said. "I set a deadline and affirmed that I would meet someone by year-end. I met Bill in October, but we didn't start dating until the following February, so when December rolled around, I thought I had failed in meeting my goal. Later, when Bill and I started dating, I realized I had, indeed, met my goal, because my goal was to *meet* someone by year-end, I didn't say anything about *dating* him by year-end. You have to be very specific when you state your goals."

DOTTIE
Give the guy a chance

Dottie, the stockbroker you met in Chapter 2, is another who believes too many women still cling to the so-called White Knight fantasy, even though they probably wouldn't admit it, even to themselves.

"Lots of women think that at a certain age, 'I deserve Mr. Right.' But who is this person who's right for you? Certainly not the White Knight you may have fantasized about when you were younger," she said. "The man you meet when you're in your 40s is not going to fulfill the fantasies you may have had when you were in high school and college. So I say, if you meet someone who's decent, take the time to get to know him. Don't reject him just because you haven't been swept off your feet. Give the guy a chance and you just might be pleasantly surprised."

Question: What was your initial reaction to your future husband?

In asking this question, I was curious to know how many of the women in the survey married men that they did not like at first or did not feel any great attraction to initially. Like Dottie, do most of them believe in giving a guy a chance even if they are not instantly attracted to him, or do they still believe in love at first sight? Just how common is so-called love at first sight? And just how reliable is it?

For seven of the Marriage 100, it was, indeed, love at first sight. But seven others never wanted to see the guy again. Overall, the vast majority (69) had favorable first impressions, while 20 had negative first impressions, and 13 were indifferent.

I'm in the majority. My initial reaction to my husband, Jerry, was that he was a nice guy, but I wasn't particularly interested in dating him. Luckily for me, I did say yes to having dinner with him to talk about two interests we shared, Spain and the bullfights. I still wasn't interested in a relationship, mainly because Jerry was in the midst of a divorce and the last thing I wanted was to get involved in someone else's divorce (my own was enough, thank you very much).

What changed my mind was a bold move on his part, one that overwhelmed me and, in a sense, swept me off my feet. It happened at New York's La Guardia Airport shortly after midnight, in the month of June. My girlfriend, Diane, and I were returning home from a four-day trip to Puerto Vallarta, Mexico, and had just arrived at La Guardia. As we're walking down the ramp toward baggage claim, who did I see standing there, with a sheepish grin on his face, but Jerry. He said, "Hello, would you like a ride?" as if this were an everyday occurrence. I was speechless. Diane was grinning from ear to ear, because during our trip I told her I had met a really nice guy—and here he was!

I remembered telling Jerry on our first dinner date that I was leaving the following week on a trip to Mexico, but I hadn't given him any details, other than the fact that our flight would arrive around midnight from Dallas. He told me later that he had called the airport to find out which flights were arriving at that time from Dallas and he took a chance on finding me, and an even bigger chance on whether I'd be happy to see him. I wasn't just happy, I was thrilled.

Jerry drove Diane and me home, dropping her off first. As he was getting her luggage out of the trunk, Diane whispered to me, "I think you have a live one." The next night Jerry and I had dinner together at a Spanish restaurant. It didn't take me long to realize that this was someone whose company I could enjoy for a long time to come.

DEE
Love at first sight

One of the lucky seven who did feel love at first sight was Dee, who fell head over heels the minute she saw her husband.

"I thought I just couldn't live without him," she said. "It was a real teenage-type reaction. I couldn't believe it! I was 40 years old and the mother of three, and here I was flipping out like a 15-year-old!"

Dee met Daniel at a dinner dance that she went to with a married couple. They had their first date two days later.

"After our first date, Daniel called and proposed marriage to me every night," she said. "He told me that he, too, had been swept off his feet." They were married six months later, the second time for both of them.

And then there's the other side of the coin—those who were not so thrilled by their first encounters with their husbands-to-be. Here's what a few had to say.

Laura
Ugh!

"I thought he was disgusting. I not only disliked him, I was repulsed by him."

That's Laura, an accountant from Iowa who wed for the third time at 48. She met Kevin, a salesman, at a friend's wedding. Laura said the main reason she was turned off was because she suspected he was on drugs, a habit she had kicked several years before. Five years later they met again at a Narcotics Anonymous meeting.

"He had been clean for three years and was a totally changed man," she said. "I fell for him hard. We went out to dinner a month later and shortly afterward I moved in with him. We were married three years after we met."

Olivia
Nice but . . .

Olivia, a publicist, who wed for the first time at 43, is one of many who is glad she gave the guy a chance. She met her husband, Herb, through a dating service, and admits she wasn't terribly impressed.

"I thought he was nice but not for me," she said. "Herb was a bit shy, not particularly good looking and still a bachelor at 45. We met for pizza on our first date and we both felt shy and awkward. But after a couple of hours we got over our mutual shyness, and I began to feel very comfortable with him.

"With Herb I learned an important lesson," she continued. "Don't automatically reject someone because he's shy and not handsome. In my younger days I would have rejected such a man. I'm so glad I took the time to get to know him, because he's turned out to be everything I've always wanted in a husband."

LINDA
Screw you

Linda, a divorced mother of four, met Don at a ski resort in Colorado, where she was conducting a survey for a ski trade association. It was definitely not love at first sight.

"He flew into Denver from the east coast and then drove to Vail in a snowstorm. By the time he finally arrived, he was in a foul mood," she said. "It was Super Bowl Sunday and all he wanted to do was get into his room and watch the game. I tried to talk to him, for my survey, as he was waiting for check-in. He was so gruff and nasty that I thought, 'Screw You!'and walked away."

Later, he apologized and they exchanged business cards. She lived in Los Angeles and he lived in Rhode Island, so she didn't think she'd ever see him again, and she didn't particularly care.

"At the time I was newly divorced and I had more guys than I knew what to do with," she said. "I was very happy being single, and I definitely didn't need a guy who lived in Rhode Island."

Don apparently was smitten and didn't see distance as too big a hurdle. He pursued her with letters, phone calls and dozens of flights on the redeye. Eventually they started a long-distance romance. When he retired he moved to Los Angeles to be with Linda. They were married four years after they met. She was 48.

MARY
He's stodgy and rigid

"When Bob and I first met, I thought he was stodgy and rigid, and much too old for me," said Mary, a secretary who wed for the second time at 46. Bob, an electrical engineer, is thirteen years older than Mary. After ten years of marriage to Bob, she sings the praises of older men and encourages other women to cast their nets for an older man.

"Men over 50 are the last of the true gentlemen," she said. "They treat you like a lady all the time. They're polite, they show you and others respect and consideration, something I think younger men have forgotten. A man in his 50s or 60s has mellowed, he's gotten to the point where he doesn't worry about much of anything, because he knows that life's too short. Their priorities are different. That's probably true with all of us. As we age, we tend to mellow, it's why older marriages work so well."

Question: List the three most important qualities you think women over 40 should look for in a prospective mate. How do these qualities differ from what you looked for when you were younger?

My main reason for asking this question was to find out if there is much disparity between the qualities women thought were important when they were younger and what they think are important now. In most cases, there was a big difference. About two-thirds of the women said that good looks, money, and sex appeal were what counted most when they were in their 20s and early 30s. But as they approached 40, they said they were ready for compatibility, a sense of humor and simple kindness.

Here are the traits that topped the list: Kindness, gentleness, honesty, and a loving nature (27 listings each); a sense of humor (26 listings); financial success and stable personality (22 listings each); self confidence, zest for life, enthusiasm, and generosity (10 listings each). The traits mentioned least were good looks (5 listings), and sexual compatibility (1 listing).

I pretty much fit in with the majority here—looks, money, and sex appeal were very important to me when I was in my 20s and thinking about marriage. By the time I reached my 40s, all of the above still mattered, but not as much as being with someone who could express his feelings and was a good listener (which was not the case with my first husband), and someone who could loosen up and be childlike. I didn't want a workaholic (never did) because I think that by the time you reach your 50s, it's more important to enjoy the money you have than to kill yourself trying to earn more than you'll probably ever need. Rhoda (below) pretty much sums up my own feelings on the subject.

RHODA
Have fun

"When you're young and want children, it's important that a man be a good provider and family-oriented," said Rhoda. "But when you reach middle age, if money is no longer a major need in your life (and it still can be, of course), then look for compatibility, integrity and someone who's fun loving." Rhoda wed for the third time at 73. She met her husband, Jules, at a party in their condo community.

CATHERINE
Think long term

"When I was in my 20s and 30s I looked for superficial things, such as looks and what type of car he drove. I didn't think about the long term, and as a result, my first two marriages ended in divorce," she said. "Now I know that what counts in the long run is health, education, common interests, and financial security." A high school teacher, Catherine met Travis, her third husband, in a personal growth workshop. She was 50 when they wed.

MONTROSE LIBRARY DISTRICT
320 So. 2nd St.
Montrose, CO 81401

Shirley
Focus on compatibility (and golf)

Another who echoes Catherine's sentiments is Shirley, a secretary from New Jersey, who wed for the second time at 47.

"Sex and good looks were what counted when I was younger," she said. "Now I couldn't care less about either. What makes for a good marriage is compatibility. Look for someone who's going to be a good companion, who shares your interests and your values—that's what lasts."

Shirley and Lou, who met at their golf club, share a passion for the sport. They spend most of their spare time at their local club, teeing off together in the warm months and, in the winter, when the greens are white (or, more likely, soggy), working together on the social committee, planning parties and other events.

Shari
Forget old views

"When I was younger, looks were very important, also religion and ethnic background. Now I say, forget all that and look for thoughtfulness, a sense of humor and competence in how he runs both his business and his personal life," said Shari. A school counselor, she wed for the second time at 48. Her husband, a physician, is Catholic, and she's Jewish.

"Who cares about the differences," she said. "We respect each other's religion, and each other's point of view. That's all that matters."

Sarah
How does he treat others?

"In my teens and 20s, looks were very important, in my 30s it was money, but in my 40s I forgot all that. I got smart and started to look for self-confidence in a man, and whether we had common interests," said Sarah, who wed for the second time at 45. "For me, a very good barometer of a man's character is whether he treats me and others with respect," she said. "Watch carefully how he treats others, especially when his guard is down and he's not trying to impress you."

RUTH
Find a grownup

"In my younger days, I wanted someone who was popular and sought after," said Ruth. "Now I would advise women to look for a man with emotional maturity, a good self-image, and a lively and interesting personality." A teacher, Ruth married for the third time at 56. She met Gordon, an engineer, at a party given by mutual friends.

Red Flag Issues

Sometimes, it's the little things that tell you the most about a person. Before you get too involved with a new man, watch and listen carefully, and be ever alert to those cues that suggest that perhaps this guy isn't for you. Several of the women mentioned small things they saw in a particular man that warned them not to go any further—red flag issues about a man's honesty, his level of generosity, and his kindness and consideration. How he treats strangers, as well as friends and family, says a lot.

He's dishonest

Gladys, who wed for the second time at 44, said she had a real eye-opener on a dinner date, her first and last with a man she initially found very attractive.

"He did something that totally turned me off," she said. "We had a very pleasant evening at a nice restaurant and I felt very positive about seeing him again. Everything seemed fine until we left the restaurant and were in the car. Then he started to laugh and told me that when the bill came, he noticed that the waitress had undercharged us, but he paid the bill without telling her she'd made a mistake. He said to me, 'That stupid waitress only charged me for one meal.' I knew then and there he wasn't for me. I once heard Maya Angelou say on TV, 'If someone tells you who they are, believe them.' Yes, and I would add, if someone shows you through his actions that he can't be trusted, believe him, he can't be trusted."

He's cheap

"If you're at McDonald's and he asks, 'How come I have to buy the dinner all the time?' Watch out. He's cheap," said Iris, who wed at 63 for the third time. "It doesn't mean he has to take you to expensive restaurants all the time, or that you can't treat him sometimes, but if he resents treating you, he's cheap and it probably carries through into other areas of his life."

He's hard to reach

In this day and age with everyone running around with cell phones and car phones, and having call-waiting, call-forwarding, you name it, beware the man who doesn't have a home phone (or tells you he doesn't). He's hiding something.

Ricky, who wed for the second time at 48, learned that lesson the hard way.

"I dated a guy for a year who did not have a telephone in his apartment. I could only reach him at his office, through his secretary. I'd been to his apartment many times, so I knew he wasn't married or living with someone, but when I'd ask why no phone, he would mumble something about not being home enough to warrant one," she said. "What was really happening is that I was one of three women he was dating 'exclusively.' He did not want one woman to call him at home when he was with another. It was also a good way to control our relationship, since I could only reach him by leaving a message with his secretary and then I'd have to wait for him to return the call. Mutual friends finally clued me in. I felt like such a fool."

He ignores his kids

"Watch how he treats his children and grandchildren, it's a prime indication of his character," said Kim, who remarried at 45. "If he's kind and caring to his family, he'll be kind and caring to yours. If he ignores them, or he's unkind to them, run."

He treats his ex badly

"Look closely at how he treats his ex because it's an indication of how he'll treat you," said Angela, who wed for the first time at 44. "If he's bitter and constantly complains about what his ex *did* to him, if he begrudges the mother of his children every penny he sends her, look out, this could be an angry man who sees women as users and takers."

He needs a housekeeper

"You might *prefer* to cook and clean, but if he *needs* you for that, beware—you might end up being the live-in maid," said Georgia, who rewed at 48.

Question: Were you searching for a husband? Why? Why not?

We all know, "Seek and Ye Shall Find." Well, it ain't necessarily so, at least when it comes to seeking a husband, if we can judge by the women in this survey. The majority, 39, said they were not searching for a mate when they met their husband. But 29 said they were. Many of the others answered with, "not sure," "maybe," "yes and no," "not consciously, but perhaps subconsciously." Most of those who said they were not looking said they were "burned out," "involved in a career," or "enjoying the single life."

JUDY
Wrapped up in work

"I was wrapped up in my career. In the back of my mind I might have wanted to find a husband, but I never gave it much thought because all of my energy went into my work," said Judy, a high school guidance counselor who was a first-time bride at 44. Not surprisingly, since work is her life, she married a co-worker, the school district superintendent, and a man as involved in his career as she is in hers.

"I was assigned to a meeting once a month in George's office. He was married when we first met, but his wife had a terminal illness and died shortly after we started working together," she said. "Several months later, George started popping into my office almost on a daily basis. Looking back on it, I realize he was calling me and dropping by a lot more than he needed to, but I was so involved with my projects that I was oblivious to it all.

"Until he made the first move, I really didn't give it much thought," she continued. "One day, at the end of a meeting, he asked me to have coffee with him. I think that's when I first got the message that he was interested. We went out for dinner shortly after that and we practically decided to get married then and there. We'd been working together for a couple years by then, so knew each other well."

Judy said one of the things that she most admired about George when she first started working with him was that he was highly respected by his colleagues.

"Watch how a man treats his employees and co-workers. This is very important," she said. "Do they like and respect him? If they do, it says a lot that's positive."

SILVIA
Ditto

Like Judy, Silvia was also a first-time bride in her 40s who was career-oriented and didn't give marriage much thought. An administrator at a federal agency in New York, Silvia was 46 when she married.

"I have always loved my work," she said. "I've been fortunate that way. When I was growing up in Indiana, my parents assumed I would marry a farmer as soon as I finished high school and settle down to have a family."

She had other ideas, and headed to New York where she got a job with a nonprofit organization and eventually worked her way up to an executive-level position. Her husband-to-be popped into her life one Sunday afternoon during a walking tour of one of New York's historic districts.

"He asked me if I'd have dinner with him after the tour. I asked him whether he was married. He said no, he was a bachelor. I said, fine, since I was single, too. We were married six months to the day," she said. "Don't worry about finding a husband. Just enjoy yourself, do what interests you, and the right man will come along. It worked for me and it can work for you."

MARCIE
Lasting scars

Marcie, like so many women, had been badly burned by past marriages and relationships and had no desire to get involved again—until she met her current husband.

"Wrong choices leave lasting scars," she said. Marcie was 45 with two grown children when she met her husband on a blind date. He was 63.

"In my two previous marriages, I married for all the wrong reasons—security, someone to love me, escape from my family," she said.

Echoing the advice of Jo, Marcie stressed the importance of holding out for a man who really wants to be your partner.

"This time I chose a man who genuinely wants to be with me and have a committed relationship," she said. "Look for that type of commitment and everything else will work itself out."

Question: What does your husband say attracted him to you?

Just what is it about these women that helped them beat the so-called marriage odds? Was it looks? Apparently not. I asked for height, weight and hair color. Very few were super-model thin. Personally, I found it a relief to know that there was no strong correlation between weight and self-confidence. The ones who described themselves as "Rubenesque" or "ample" did not mention their size as being a problem in meeting men. This is not to say you should let yourself go. But I don't think most men are turned off by women with a few extra pounds, any more than most of us are turned off by slightly overweight men.

Remember that old saying, "The fastest way to a man's heart is through his stomach"? Not true, judging from the Marriage 100. Only four of them listed their cooking skills as something that enticed their husbands into matrimony. Some women mentioned "my legs" or "my breasts" when asked what attracted their husbands. Several said "my looks." Mostly it was said tongue-in-cheek. As one woman put it, "He said it was my big boobs, but I don't believe him because I hid them well and it was a long time before he saw them."

BECKY
My jacuzzi

Becky's husband, Fred, said he was attracted to her vivacious personality, her looks, and the fact that she was independent, with a good job (teacher) and her own home (with jacuzzi). They met at a 30th anniversary college reunion in the Midwest. She lived in Phoenix, he lived in Los Angeles.

"We didn't know each other in college," she said. "After I got to know him, I was really impressed by the fact that he had positive views on marriage and wasn't afraid of commitment. I was quite taken with him." They were married eight months later, both for the second time. She was 52, he was 51.

JOYCE
My baroque figure

"He says it was my 'broad-based cultural background' and my 'wide interests and ability to converse on many subjects,' but I think it was really my red bathing suit and my broad-based baroque figure." That's Joyce, a nurse, who met Ken, an English teacher, on a weekend with mutual friends on Fire Island (more about that in Chapter 5). She was 50 when they wed, her second marriage, his fourth.

"What really impressed me about Ken is how much he genuinely likes women. He looks beyond a woman's face or figure. He sees the person inside the body. He's the first man I know who can do that; most seem to focus on looks, at least in the beginning. Hopefully there are more men like Ken out there, if so, grab them."

Question: What interests, hobbies, etc. do you and your husband share? What interests do you not share?

Of the 100 women, only nine said they and their husbands do everything together. Two others said they don't share any interests with their husbands. The majority have long lists of interests they share with their husbands, and an equally long list of interests they don't share. Live and let live seems to be the norm.

While it's always good advice to look for someone who wants to participate in as many of your interests as possible, the fact is that a lot of couples have perfectly happy marriages with only one or two mutual interests. By the time you reach your 40s, you're probably not going to suddenly become a football fan if you weren't one already. And if you try to fake it (as all those old "How To Get Your Man" books used to advise), you'll live to regret it.

If you married a man like my husband, for example, and you fibbed about loving sports, you'd end up spending Saturday and Sunday afternoons and Monday evenings in front of the TV watching football, baseball, soccer and (God have mercy) golf tournaments. For me, having to watch a golf tournament on TV would be a special form of torture. For my husband, it's a thrilling display of skill and concentration.

On the other hand, my favorite Sunday afternoon activity is sitting in one of the dozens of tiny theaters in Greenwich Village or SoHo and watching a Greek tragedy unfold (which others might consider a special form of torture) or Ibsen's *Doll House* for the umpteenth time. At first, my husband, bless his soul, used to come with me. I thought he enjoyed it. But about six months into our marriage, he announced that he wanted to spend his weekend afternoons watching sports on TV, not at theater matinees. That was OK with me since I was used to doing things on my own. Now I go off to my matinees almost every Sunday, and he watches his golf tournaments. And we're both happy.

Another example is the bullfight club. When I tell women I met my husband at a bullfight club, sometimes they want to come to a meeting with me, not because they're interested in bullfighting, but because they think there might be some interesting single men there. I say, OK, but then I ask if they are willing to sit in a room full of men smoking cigars, watching videotapes from Spain or Latin America, that show, up close and personal, a matador killing a bull (or a bull goring a matador). Do they want to listen to endless talk about which matador performed the best cape passes, which one had an especially bad time of it, and which ranches are breeding the best fighting bulls? And all this before, during, and after dinner? In other words, you'd better have a genuine interest in the subject at hand or you're in for a boring time, at the very least.

The bottom line is this, whatever your special interests, passions, or hobbies, the chances are you're not going to give them up just because they don't happen to interest a particular male, or vice versa. Nor should you. And the same holds true for him.

FAY
Very few shared interests

One of those who shares almost no interests with her husband is Fay, who wed for the second time at 45. She answered, "Very little" to the question of common interests.

She and her husband, Ron, both enjoy an active retirement (she was an interior decorator, Ron, a banker), but in totally different ways.

"Ron and I go our separate ways during the day. He goes to a local college to a program for retired professionals that meets daily and I go to my art classes and whatever else interests me," she said. "We meet for dinner and discuss our day. He's interested in hearing what I do, but he's not involved. I was interested for a while in the program he's taking, but I didn't want to be committed to something so structured. He needs the structure, I don't. We give each other free rein, and it works just fine."

SANDRA
Ballet for her, opera for him

Sandra is another woman with a happy marriage despite few shared interests. A mother of two, she wed for the second time at 50.

"We don't have many shared interests, except for my children and grandchildren. He doesn't have children of his own, so he's taken to mine and is very close to them," she said. "Otherwise, we pursue separate interests. My favorite pastimes are swimming laps daily and going to the ballet. He loves spectator sports, especially football, and he also loves the opera (I don't). We have a deal, I don't drag him to the ballet or the swimming pool and he doesn't drag me to the opera or the football games."

GLORIA
Strange bedfellows

Gloria, a twice-divorced political activist of the liberal persuasion, was 40 when she wed David, a conservative business executive.

"We share a love of politics, though we rarely agree," she said. Where they do agree is their commitment to family (two kids each by previous marriages), their careers (she's an administrative assistant, he heads a marketing firm), books, and music. Their taste in music is as different as their politics—she's into hard rock and he's an opera lover. For Gloria the differences don't matter.

"What matters is that your companion is supportive of you, and you of him—and as long as both of you understand that there will be adjusting and compromising, the rewards are overwhelmingly gratifying."

LOIS AND CHARLES, CARLA AND BILL
Togetherness

Earlier, you met Lois (the hiker, who wed for the first time at 44) and Carla (retired saleswoman, who wed for the third time at 60). Both said they share everything with their husbands.

"We do everything together—hiking, working out at a gym, ballroom dancing," said Lois. But even Lois draws the line somewhere. "He likes to shop at Home Depot, I don't. That he does by himself."

Carla goes one better, "We do everything together—golfing, tennis, dancing, traveling, painting, watching football (although he watches more football than I do). We even go shopping together."

Question: How important is sex in this marriage?

Slightly over half (55) of the women answered this question with "Very important," "Very special," or "It's better than in my first marriage." Seventeen said it wasn't important at all and, in some cases, nonexistent. Three women said their sex drive was low and blamed menopause, while others said they enjoyed sex more since going through menopause, mainly because there were fewer stresses in the relationship and the kids were out of the house. A few said it was more important to their husbands than to them, and one said her husband's lack of interest in sex was very bothersome. But whether sex was important or nonexistent, virtually all of the women said plain, old-fashioned affection, such as cuddling, holding hands, and kissing, was just as important as intercourse, and it went a long way in helping them feel good about themselves and their marriage.

KATHLEEN
It's fun again

You can almost picture Kathleen jumping up and down and shouting with joy, "The kids are grown and gone—it's fun again! We can be spontaneous, anywhere in the house." Kathleen married Hal when she was 41 and he was 54. It was her second marriage, his third.

KAREN, RHODA, IRIS, AND MADDIE
Sexy grandmas

Some of the women who are most enthusiastic about sex are grandmothers who managed to surprise even themselves with the great sex they are enjoying in their current marriage.

Karen is one of them. She's the widow who met her second husband at her first husband's funeral. She was 67 and the mother of four and grandmother of 10 when she married Jack, 73.

"Jack and I started dating about six months after we met. My children and grandchildren didn't know about it—it was none of their business. Jack didn't move in right away, but he was around a lot. If I was invited to a dinner or other event and could take an escort, I'd take him; otherwise, I'd go alone and leave him at home. He'd spend the night, and we'd often have to jump out of bed and throw on our clothes in the morning when one of my kids dropped by unannounced. They didn't have a clue."

Rhoda was 73 and Jules was 80 when they wed, each for the third time. To the great surprise of both of them, sex quickly became a very important part of their life together.

"It is a surprising and delightful passion for us both," she said. "Neither one of us thought this could be possible. But why shouldn't older couples enjoy sex? Unfortunately, grown children have difficulty thinking of their parents as being sexual. Sex among the elderly seems to be very disturbing to a lot of people."

Another who is enjoying great sex is Iris. Apparently a late bloomer, she said, "I didn't get interested in sex until I was 60. That's when I started dating Michael. Sex is very important to both of us." Iris was 63 and Michael was 67 when they wed, she for the third time, he for the second time.

Also happily surprised was Maddie, a mother of six and grandmother of five. She wed Fred when she was 68 and he was 71.

"Sex is very important in this marriage, although I didn't really expect it to be," she said.

More comments about sex

- "It's important, but cuddling is more important."
- "More important than in my first marriage. Now it's meaningful, spontaneous, expressive of happy, intimate feelings, not just a routine that people easily fall into."
- "It's very important and now we have the time and inclination for it."
- "Not as important as in my first marriage, where sex was the main interest."
- "It's important, but companionship is more important to us."
- "At first it *was* the marriage, now it's not so important."
- "It's a lovely part of our marriage."
- "The physical gratification is truly fabulous, but the mental closeness and commitment we feel toward each other is even better."

Question: Is religion important in your marriage?

When I asked this question, I really didn't expect many women to give religion much weight, but maybe that's because I'm not religious myself. I was surprised to find how many women said that religion is, indeed, very important to them and how many are actively involved with their religion or are on a spiritual path of some sort.

One woman, who met her husband through a Jewish dating service said, "My religion is very important to me, I only wanted to marry a fellow Jew." Another said, "I'm not very religious, but I wouldn't have married him if he weren't Catholic."

Fifty-four of the women said religion is very important to them and believe it's a strong component of a happy marriage. But if you're not religious, don't despair—another 42 said religion was not at all important to them or to their husbands. The rest were either lukewarm on the subject or said religion mattered to one partner or the other, but that the differences weren't a problem.

CASSIE
Temple on Friday, church on Sunday

"I'm Jewish, he's Lutheran, and we're both very strong in our religious beliefs," said Cassie, who wed for the second time at 47. "We've learned to be respectful of each other's differences. It's also taught us to compromise. We attend services with each other—temple on Friday night, church on Sunday. I think respect for the beliefs of others and a faith of your own is very, very important—not only for a happy marriage, but for a happy life."

TERRY
Off to India

"I'm spiritual, he's not, but I think he's more interested in hearing about my beliefs than he lets on," said Terry, the divorced mother of two who wed the retired Army officer (Chapter 2). She's a student of Vedanta, a branch of Hinduism, and occasionally goes off to an ashram in India. "He's extremely supportive of my beliefs. I've been to India five times and it's OK with Ed. He has no interest in joining me, but he doesn't mind if I go alone."

ROSE
United in faith

Rose met Jay when they both sang in the church choir. Their first date was attending church together on Sunday. They are both deeply religious and committed to their Christian faith.

"We agree to obey God's word only. We are united in our faith, which I think is the most important thing you can share with your spouse." She was 45 and he was 49 when they wed—it was her second marriage, his third.

EILEEN
He's high Mass, she's folk Mass

"We're both Irish Catholic, although I was a lapsed Catholic when I met Kevin. We go to church together every Sunday, but I go downstairs to the folk Mass and he stays upstairs for high Mass. Luckily, the two Masses are conducted at the same time," said Eileen. She's the one who met her husband through a tennis group and wed for the first time at 47.

"I think having similar backgrounds, especially having the same religion, definitely helps keep a marriage on track," she said.

GLADYS
Religion creates a bond

"Sharing a religion is really important in a marriage. It gives you a closeness, a camaraderie. People who aren't of the same faith don't quite have the same bond. There's always a schism."

Gladys speaks from experience. A member of the Church of Jesus Christ of Latter Day Saints, she wed an atheist the first time around.

"Although the marriage lasted twenty years, there was a definite void there. I'm certain that our lack of a common faith played a big role in our marriage being empty and its ending in divorce," she said. "I was very active in my church and he was supportive of that, but I was never able to share my religious viewpoints with him and he never went to church activities with me."

Gladys met her second husband, Raul, at a church singles meeting. They were both 44 when they wed. He's as committed to their faith as she is.

"If religion is important to you, then it's important that you find a partner who'll share your spiritual beliefs, whatever they may be," she said. "In this marriage, whatever touches us spiritually, we share with each other and that helps to forge a very strong bond."

The common thread in all of this is that there is no one way of doing things. Do you meet men by looking or by not looking? Do you try to find someone to share most of your interests, or someone that will allow you to do your own thing, while he does his? And when it comes to sex, just how important is it? Important for some, but not for others. At least 80 percent of the women emphasized that the one thing that's clear is that *you* must be clear on who you are and what you want in a marriage. Believe in yourself was another strong message. As one woman said, "In order for something to happen, you have to believe that it's possible."

Listen Up

Here's some added advice from the Marriage 100. A lot of it may seem obvious, but how often have we ignored or forgotten the obvious, much to our dismay? Below is a refresher course, compliments of these women, of lessons often learned the hard way.

Be open to new types. Old ways of thinking usually lead to the same old results. Try looking at the men who come into your life with new eyes, and be open to new types of men. Several of the women admitted to having a deep prejudice against men over 35 who had never married, yet 18 of them married such men. Madeline was 41 and William, 43, when they wed, both for the first time: "William was so normal, that's what attracted me." Olivia, who was 43 and her husband 49 when they wed, both for the first time, said, "You need to consider men you might have rejected earlier. You'd be surprised how many good men are out there who've never been married." Bobbie, who was 42 when she married a 41-year-old bachelor, echoed the same advice: "Be open to men who are different from the types that previously attracted you." The advice from Liz, who wed for the second time at 40, is, "Leave yourself open for change and new people, do things you enjoy while seeking a partner, keep active and *smile*."

Give the guy a chance. Right on the heels of "Be open to new types" is, "Get rid of the romantic notion of love at first sight." Yes, it happens; seven of the women attest to that. But seven others never wanted to see the guy again and many more were indifferent ("He was too quiet, not my type"). Remember, 20 of the 100 women originally had negative reactions to their future husbands and 13 were completely indifferent. One important lesson that emerged: Give the guy a chance—that's what 33 of them did and they're not sorry.

Get a life. As one woman said, "Stop looking for men all the time. If you spend most of your time shopping, life will pass you by." Another said, "Get a life and then invite men into it."

Get in touch with your needs. You can't know what works for you until you are in touch with your needs. So many of the women said one of the reasons their earlier marriages failed was because they entered them not really knowing who they were and what they wanted. Find out what you really want in a relationship today, not what is expected of you or what you thought you needed in the past.

Trust your instincts. "If getting married is right for you, you just know it," said one. Another said, "Don't settle for anything other than what you dream of. I've married just to marry, I've married for security, and I've married for love. When there is love all things are attainable and possible. Without it, nothing else works."

Know when to run. "If he was unfaithful to his prior wife, chances are good he will be unfaithful to you," said one. Others warned, "Do not marry anyone who tries to dominate you," and "Watch out for men who say they want a wife, but what they really want is a housekeeper or a mother."

Now that these women have given you their opinions on many different issues, from religion to what to look for (and avoid) in a man, let's move from the head to the heart and see what they *felt* when they found their true love and marriage loomed near. It wasn't all lovey-dovey, believe me.

CHAPTER 4

Am I Ready?

Everything is good in its season.

—ITALIAN PROVERB

As much as you may think you want to marry or remarry, don't be surprised if red lights flash and bells go off somewhere deep inside you at the mere thought of making a lifelong commitment to someone. This is especially true if you've been there before and the outcome wasn't so great. Change is rarely easy and even a positive change can be positively traumatic.

Whether you fit the stereotype of an independent, never-married career woman, a gun-shy divorcee, or a lonely widow, you're probably going to have some second thoughts about getting married and, chances are, you haven't reached age 40 or 50 without some battle scars.

I myself fit all three categories. I was independent, I was gun-shy, and sometimes I was lonely for the special type of commitment that usually only comes with marriage. So was I thrilled when my husband asked me to marry him? No. I panicked. I had several full-scale anxiety attacks. Sometimes, in the middle of the night, I would wake up in a cold sweat and wonder, could I share my space? Was I too set in my ways? Could I learn to function as part of a couple after nearly twenty-five years of functioning as a single? Was I ready for marriage? Would I ever be ready?

I didn't exactly rush into things. Jerry and I lived together (well, almost) for three years. I kept my own apartment, with the excuse that I needed office space. Now I know better—I was kidding myself. What I really needed was an escape hatch—just in case. For me, having an out was important because I'm a lone wolf at heart, used to living alone and working alone. It allowed me to relax and ease into the relationship, and for three years that's exactly what I did.

In talking to other women, I found that I wasn't alone in having deep second thoughts about getting married. When you're older, it's natural to fear losing hard-won control over your life. This is especially true of those of us who came of age in the '50s, when we were expected to let men take the lead—at least that's how I was raised. Also, the idea of too much "togetherness" scared me, probably another throwback to the '50s when so many women's magazines stressed that. Even then, I shuddered at the thought. I still do. Togetherness, for me, translates into everything being one big compromise ("We'll see the Arnold Schwarzenegger movie Friday night and attend the ballet Saturday night—and we'll each be bored silly one of those two nights.") But that's just one of my own personal, red-button issues. There were many other issues that gave women pause ("He's so messy," "Are we on the same wavelength?" "I need my space") that we'll look at in this chapter. Here's a sampling of what drove others into anxiety attacks, feelings of impending doom, or serious second thoughts as marriage loomed near. We'll look at some of these feelings from the different perspectives of the first-time bride, divorcee, and widow.

Taking the Plunge: First-Timers

You watched your friends take the plunge years ago. Now you watch their kids march down the aisle. Wasn't it only yesterday you were a bridesmaid for today's mother of the bride? If you're a baby boomer or older, chances are that most of the women you grew up with opted for marriage and motherhood right out of high school or college. Now you've met someone special and it's your turn to march down the aisle, literally or figuratively.

Of the Marriage 100, 19 were first-time brides and of these, 17 were in their 40s when they wed; one was in her 50s, and one, in her 60s. Why did they wait? Three reasons top the list:

- They liked their independence.
- They felt burned out from previous relationships and were reluctant to try again.
- They were too involved with work, travel, and other pursuits to bother looking.

When they did decide to marry, all 19 put on the brakes and refused to be rushed. Most dated their husbands for two or more years before they wed, and all but four lived with them first.

PAT
Get past your fears

Pat, a marketing executive, was 40 when she married for the first time. She's typical of many successful career women who wanted to marry but never spent much time looking for men or worrying about it.

"Was I happy being single? I think it depended on the day of the week," she said. "Overall, I'd say, yes, I was happy. I had a job I loved, I owned my own home, traveled a lot, and was pretty much footloose and fancy free. Although I rarely thought about marriage, I knew in the back of my mind I wanted to marry eventually, or at least have a permanent relationship with someone."

Over the years she had her share of relationships that fizzled. "I was engaged right out of college, but backed out a few weeks before the wedding. Later, I lived with a guy for a year, but that didn't work out either," she said.

"After that one broke up, I became very anxious. I took stock. I was 31, and at that time I wanted kids. I wasn't married, two serious relationships hadn't worked out, and I was starting to wonder if there was something wrong with me," she continued. "Gradually, I accepted the idea of being single for the rest of my life. By the time I was 35 or 36, my attitude was more like, 'Well if it happens, it happens. I'm not unhappy with my life.'"

She met her husband at work when he was put in charge of a new division and she was loaned to him to help set up a marketing plan. ("It was instant friendship," she recalls.) They worked together for two years before they had their first date (a disaster, see Chapter 6), and lived together for another year before they wed.

Pat said a lot of her anxieties about giving up her single lifestyle surfaced when she sold her house and moved in with Pete, her future husband.

"After ten years of living alone, I found that living with someone was very difficult," she said. "I had a full-blown anxiety attack right after I sold my house. Suddenly it hit me, 'I don't have a place that's mine anymore!' Oh Lord, that was the scariest of all."

Pat, like Gerry, said she dealt with her anxieties by reading self-help books and heading back into the classroom for self-awareness courses, including one on Transactional Analysis.

"These types of classes are inexpensive and very helpful," she said. "Many are taught by psychologists, ministers, and others with insight into the human condition. You meet people you can share your thoughts with, and you learn techniques, such as meditation, for getting past your fears or mental blocks. If you don't have time for classes, you can find lots of this type of material in public libraries."

Pat warns that if you're used to being in control of your life, you'll probably have to deal with some anxiety attacks when you finally decide to take the plunge, but not to worry, it's all part of the letting-go process.

"It's very interesting to go from being single, where you have control of everything you do, to suddenly needing your husband's signature on important documents, such as insurance or tax forms," she said. "It really hit home for me at tax time the first year we were married. I've always done my own taxes and volunteered to work on our joint return because I'm very comfortable with tax forms and very competent in this area.

"One evening, as I was working on our first joint return, Pete took the tax forms away from me to check my accuracy. I thought, 'Wait a minute! I've been doing this for twenty years without anyone looking over my shoulder.' I know that might sound arrogant, but I had a strong emotional reaction the first time it happened. It reminded me that I was no longer autonomous."

ERICA
Let him be a slob (up to a point)

For ten years, Erica, an interior designer, had an on-again, off-again relationship with her future husband, Brian. Neither had been married before, both were in their late 40s, highly independent, and used to living alone. This was a case of Ms. Super Neat meets Mr. Major Messy.

"There were a lot of issues I had to work out in my own head before I decided to marry him," she said. "None the least of which is the fact that I'm very neat and well organized—I like everything in its place. He's a pack rat and never throws things out. He saves everything—newspapers, magazines, books he'll never read again. I wondered if I could live with that."

Before they became engaged, they decided to try living together to see whether it could work out. He moved into her one-bedroom, exquisitely decorated apartment, a place filled with white carpets and white furniture, and shimmering with silver candlesticks, crystal goblets and fine china. Would her beer drinking, fun-loving, lifelong bachelor survive in this environment? Would she survive his sloppiness, his mania for saving things? The answer to both is yes. They lived together for a year and then had an old-fashioned church wedding, where close friends and families breathed a collective sigh of relief.

"The place is a lot messier now, with piles of old magazines and at least twenty books strewn about," she said. "But I've mellowed. I learned I could live with it—and Brian really is trying to be a bit more tidy."

ANNETTE
Take a chance

Annette, the novelist and college teacher you met earlier, is one of those independent types who never wanted to marry. She surprised even herself when she tied the knot at 44. And she did something she swore she'd never do—she married outside her race. Annette is African-American, her husband, Marv, is a blue-eyed blond of German descent.

"My friends, both black and white, were in absolute shock when I told them I was getting married—shock that I, of all people, was getting married, and shock that I was marrying a white man," she said. "Mostly they were shocked that I was getting married, regardless of race, because I never showed any interest in marriage—I was blissfully happy with my single life."

Annette was Marv's secretary for twelve years before she quit to work on her novel.

"We worked together and were very close friends, but I never thought of him romantically," she continued. "Not only was he the wrong race for me, but for the entire time I worked for him, he was married with three children at home."

For several years, Annette spent her evenings and weekends with her true love—a novel she was writing about growing up in the South. Eventually she accumulated enough money to quit her job and write full-time, with a little teaching on the side. A few months later, a friend from the office called to tell her that Marv had split up with his wife and they were getting divorced.

"I was stunned. I said to my friend, 'You gotta be kidding. He must be having a hard time because he's a very uptight person. I'm sure he doesn't know what's going on,'" she said.

She called the office and offered her condolences, and they promised to stay in touch, primarily because she was close to his three children. Months later, after hearing him complain, for the umpteenth time, about existing on TV dinners, Annette invited Marv over for a home-cooked meal.

"After that, he started dropping by for dinner on a fairly regular basis, but it was all platonic," she said. "Even though we were good friends and had a lot in common, it would never have occurred to me to go after him. One evening I even tried to give him advice on how to get back with his wife and fix his marriage. He told me, 'I don't need to fix it. I spent all these years trying to get out of it; I'm not about to get back into it.'"

Two weeks later, he asked her out on a date, but she turned him down on the basis that she didn't get involved romantically with white men.

"He was really surprised, and said, 'What are you talking about? You could be green and it wouldn't make any difference to me. I don't like you because you're black or in spite of your being black. It's who you are that I'm attracted to.' That was the beginning of my falling in love with him," she said. "I guess it happened between us because I wasn't trying to make it work, because I didn't care if it worked out. It just slowly evolved from a friendship into a full-blown romance."

Seven months after he moved into her condo and they started living together, Annette was still in no hurry to get married.

"I was happy with the status quo," she said. "I wanted to finish my novel before I did anything else with my life, and I didn't see any real reason to marry. Was I deliberately dragging my feet? Probably. I was happy being single, I wasn't so sure about being equally happy in marriage. But Marv was adamant about our getting married. He's old fashioned that way. He said I wasn't writing fast enough and insisted I set a three-month deadline for finishing the book so we could get married."

It worked; she finished her novel and got married, both right on deadline.

"It was hard for me to take that step into matrimony, because there were things I didn't really know about men. I grew up in a house full of women. I had never lived with a man. All my life I avoided trying to understand this thing called 'man.' I knew nothing about how men acted, or why."

Annette said that she jumped in anyway and for her, the greatest reward in being married is "being able to give who you are and not having to worry about what the other person is going to do with it. It's knowing he's not going to take advantage of you when your guard is down.

"I'm a very caring and giving person and I can get pissed off if I figure I'm giving more than the other person. I would walk away from relationships like that," she said. "Marv is different. He's sensitive and caring and wants to keep me happy. I care as much about him as I care about myself, and I know he feels the same way about me. I'm so glad I was willing to take a chance with him."

VIRGINIA
Face tough issues or sink

Virginia, who wed for the first time at 41, had a lot of emotional issues to work out before she felt she was ready for marriage.

She feels very strongly that if either partner comes to a marriage carrying a lot of emotional baggage, the problems have to be faced or they will probably sink the marriage.

"Make sure you've dealt with past problems and make sure your husband-to-be has, too. This is especially important if either of you come from a dysfunctional family where you suffered a lot of abuse, physical or emotional," she said. "If that's the case with him, and he hasn't dealt with painful issues, it's vital that he be willing to enter marriage counseling or work with a therapist—before you marry."

Virginia knows what she's talking about. She herself is a survivor of sibling incest.

"I had a lot of sexual problems to work through before I could have a good sexual relationship," she said.

"Sex is a very important part of this marriage. It never worked for me in past relationships because of the incest issues, but I've undergone years of therapy and have worked very hard to heal those wounds."

Because of her troubled background and the fact that her husband, Will, has family issues of alcoholism, co-dependence, and depression, she insisted that they both undergo marriage counseling for a month before their marriage.

"When you've dealt with the past, you're less apt to repeat old, destructive patterns and you're much more apt to attract a man who's loving and supportive and right for you," she said. "But it takes a lot of intensive therapy and inner work before you get to that point. Pre-marriage counseling is very helpful, but it can't end there. Getting rid of destructive patterns is an ongoing struggle. Will has been in therapy for a year for depression. In so many ways he is perfect for me and has the qualities I highly value, but life with him has been difficult at times. You have to know what you're getting into and be willing to deal with it."

Here I Go Again: Divorce and Remarriage

Divorce, like childbirth, is a remarkable thing. It seems, no matter how painful, how prolonged, or how costly, women are usually willing to try again—and again.

Of the Marriage 100, 62 had at least one divorce behind them. Of these, 39 were in their second marriage, 22 were twice-divorced and in their third marriage, and one intrepid soul had gone through four divorces and was in her fifth, and happiest, marriage. All but nine had children.

LENORE
Take a deep breath and jump in

You'd probably have to flip a coin to determine which of the Marriage 100 were more nervous over the idea of getting married—the first-time brides or the divorcees.

"Was I anxious? You bet. I said to a friend of mine, who came from California for the wedding, 'What if I'm not going to be happy?' My friend replied, 'Why should you be happy? I've been miserable for twenty years.'"

That's Lenore and that was twenty years ago when she was 41, the mother of three young girls, and getting married for the second time.

"My first big anxiety attack was a week before the wedding," she continued. "I kept asking myself, 'What am I letting my kids in for, what if I fail again, and if I do fail, how do I get out of it this time?' All those thoughts kept running through my head like a tune you can't shake."

Lenore said much of her anxiety came from the fact that the breakup of her first marriage was very ugly and left some permanent scars.

"We fought over everything. He even threatened to fight me for custody of the kids if I didn't give in to some of his financial demands," she said. "I wondered if I could ever go through that again. But somehow I managed to calm down and go through with it. This time it worked out and we've survived to celebrate our twentieth wedding anniversary.

"Remarriage is a big step, especially if you have children at home. You're bound to be nervous, but take a deep breath and jump in anyway," she said, adding that even her California friend has found happiness. "After forty years with the same guy, she's finally admitting they're happy together."

Georgia
Don't be too needy

Georgia, a physical therapist from Minneapolis, was one of the last people her friends thought would remarry. After two turbulent marriages and three stormy relationships, she lived alone for fifteen years and loved it. In 1993 she embarked on her third marriage with a man who had been her patient for a year. He was 41 and it was his first marriage, she was 48.

"I had given up on the notion that Mr. Right existed. My marriages and love affairs were all filled with knock-downs and drag-outs, so I was quite content to be alone and date only casually. When you've been in a war zone for several years, it's good to finally have peace and quiet."

At least that's how she felt until she met Kyle, an auto mechanic.

"At first he was just another patient to me," she said. "Because of his work, he often had grease and dirt on his clothes and hands, and he smelled of sweat. I never looked at him as a potential partner. In fact, I was initially somewhat repulsed by him." All that changed one day when he invited her out for pizza and she found they had a lot in common and were very compatible.

Georgia believes too much weight is placed on the importance of pairing and, like most of the Marriage 100, believes that your best defense against picking the wrong man is to be self-sufficient and independent.

"Sure, it's nice to have a partner, but it's much better to be alone if a particular relationship creates too many stresses in your life," she said. "If you can be comfortable with who you are, then perhaps you can make room for another person. Men don't want someone who's too needy, financially or emotionally. Remember, though, he too must be self-sufficient.

"In other words," she said, "two adults over 40 will be happiest together if each is mature enough not to suck the life out of the other."

ALICE
Give and demand respect

No one can blame Alice for not trying. At 51, after four divorces, she married for the fifth and last time. Alice has two daughters by her first marriage, and one grandchild. She wed Brad, her fifth husband, in 1982.

"This marriage is not only the longest of my five marriages, but also the happiest," she said. "With this one I put up with less bullshit. I give more respect and I get more respect."

They met through a guy she had hired to do some work for her on a rambling Victorian house in Brooklyn that she was converting into rental property. Brad, a marketing executive who was newly divorced, was looking for part-time work to help with alimony and child-support payments. She took one look at him and hired him immediately.

"When I decided to marry again, my main concern was being certain I could maintain my current lifestyle, my personal space, and my individuality," she said. "Too many women seem willing to give up their individuality and things that are important to them when they marry.

"My life before I met my husband was the same as it is today," she continued. "That's an important point and a positive point. If I want to do something or I want to go somewhere, I just do it. I give my husband the same freedom. It's a mistake to submerge your own feelings to try to meet the expectations of your husband. Sooner or later you'll resent it."

Two more Alice-isms:

"Be up front at the beginning of a relationship. Tell him, 'This is what I do, this is who I am. If you don't like it, it's going to have to be your problem.'

"Be honest about what you like and what you don't like. Be willing to say, 'I love you but I don't love baseball, so go without me and have a great time.'"

ARLENE
Uproot the bitterness

Arlene, who wed for the second time at 52, believes it's very important to do two things—put bitterness over past relationships behind you, and be certain you and your future husband are on the same wavelength in matters that are important to both of you.

"Many women over 40 who have been married once or twice and are single again feel bitter toward men and are very reluctant to try again," she said. "I think there is a growing sense in women of my age group that men are too unpredictable and unreliable, and that it hurts too much to get involved and risk being rejected again. But if you can put the hurt and disappointment behind you, you'll be more open to meeting someone who won't hurt or reject you.

"It may sound trite, but a positive outlook on life is also very important," she continued. "Develop a sense of pride and self-worth in who you are and what you are capable of doing on your own. Most importantly, you must work on putting the past and its failures and disappointments behind you, and start looking forward to enjoying life with a new partner."

Arlene said that once you meet your intended, be sure to spend a lot of time together and really thrash things out.

"Don't close your eyes to significant differences; they can eventually become major problems in a marriage," she said. "The best way to know if you're ready for marriage is by spending a lot of time with your future husband. You must know for sure that both of you are marrying for the same reasons, whatever they may be."

Arlene also emphasized the importance of two other things—having similar goals and having the same understanding of the word "sharing."

"You must have similar goals and plans for the future and determine in advance whether you both have the same idea of what it means to share responsibilities," she said. "The word 'sharing' can mean many different things to different people, so be sure you're both in sync on this. Also, if you have children and grandchildren, it's especially important that you discuss and agree in advance on the level of involvement that you will have with each other's families."

Arlene's first marriage ended in divorce after twenty years and five children. Like so many women, she hung in there until the children were grown.

"My first marriage was primarily to have and raise a family," she said. "As the kids began to grow up and leave home, my husband and I were faced with the fact that we had to change gears and learn to enjoy each other's company and share each other's interests. That's when we realized that we were on two different paths, had two different sets of friends and different ways of enjoying ourselves. It was the beginning of the end. We decided we would both be better off not living together, since, with the children grown, we had absolutely nothing in common anymore."

Arlene, who had been single and content about it for ten years, met her current husband, Jim, on a blind dinner date set up by her daughter (more about that in Chapter 5).

Those of you who may think that having children is a handicap in meeting men, think again.

One of the major attractions between Jim and Arlene was the fact that both have large families and are very much involved with their children and grandchildren. Between the two of them they have twelve children and eighteen grandchildren. This time around, however, Arlene made certain that the focus is on her marriage, not her children.

"My marriage to Jim is primarily a partnership where we care for and take care of each other," she said. "Though we are each very much involved with our families, they are not the main focus of our relationship. The main focus is our reaching retirement age together and being free to enjoy this part of our lives together, pursuing our mutual interests."

Terry
Take a giant leap of faith

"Nervous? Both of us were so nervous that when we drove to Reno to get married, we chain-smoked all the way, for five hours. When we finally got to Reno, Ed was so nervous he drove the wrong way on a one-way street. This was a big decision for both of us—for me, because I had one divorce behind me and swore I would never remarry, and for him, because he'd already had two flops."

That's Terry the real estate broker you first met in Chapter 2, who remarried at 41. When she wed Ed she had two teenagers at home and Ed had two children from two different ex-wives, one a teenager, one a toddler, both living with their mothers.

"Why did I do it? It was a giant leap of faith," she admitted. "But nothing ventured, nothing gained. Ed is the only man I ever met who understands me, and he's the only man I truly understand. He has qualities I admire so much in people—he's understanding, compassionate, and has such clear vision. At work, he's the one everyone goes to with their problems. And the sex is great. So, why not get married?"

JOYCE
What's the worst that can happen?

"Early on, as I was casting my lot with this guy, I kept thinking, 'Suppose it doesn't work out? What if he's not as nice as he seems? What if he doesn't like my kids, or vice versa?' Finally I told myself, 'So, what if it doesn't work out, what's the worse that can happen? You'll be alone. You're alone now. If it doesn't work out, you're back to square one.'" Joyce rewed at 50 and hasn't regretted it one bit.

"I was recovering from a particularly nasty divorce when I met Ken," she continued. "While I was open to new relationships, I had no intention of remarrying for a long, long time. When I told my kids, who were grown with children of their own, that Ken and I were going to be married, they were wary at first because I had only been divorced from my first husband for a year and a half. They were afraid it might be a rebound marriage. They thought we should just live together.

"It's funny, when you're young you worry about what your parents think and when you're older you worry about what your grown kids think—and here are mine urging us to live together, not marry. Not exactly the advice my parents would have given me," said Joyce. They did live together for four months, and it was Ken who insisted they marry.

"Your fears are natural, but don't let them hold you back," she said. "My advice? Absolutely do it, take the risk. What do you have to lose?"

Good-Bye Widowhood

Not surprisingly, the widows reported the least amount of stress when they remarried. Among the Marriage 100, 21 were widows and most of them seemed to slip easily into another marriage. Many said it was because they had happy memories of their past marriages and were used to having children or grandchildren around much of the time. Some, however, admitted they learned to really enjoy being on their own and not having to take care of a spouse or a house full of children, and that the thought of remarriage did, indeed, give them pause.

Dolores

If you don't bend, you break

Dolores is typical of the widows with happy memories. She met her current husband, John, at a Bible study group. At the time, she was 64 and had three children and one grandchild. Although she was close to her family, she wanted to remarry and have a man to share her life with again.

"After nine years as a widow I was getting very lonely for companionship," she said. "I wasn't looking too much—you can get into so much trouble doing that."

She married John, a widower, six months after they met in a weekly Bible study group. Both were lonely and wanted to remarry.

"Companionship is the real plus in an older marriage, but it doesn't come without a price," she said. "We both had some adjusting to do. Because we'd both lived alone for several years after our spouses died, we were used to having lots of space of our own. After a few months I adjusted to having less space, but I still insist on having my own time and some space to do the things that interest me. I have a room of my own for reading, watching TV, using my sewing machine. I can enjoy my hobbies without being bothered. That's more important to me now than it was in my first marriage."

Dolores feels many women who say they want to marry are so set in their ways that it's hard for them to connect with men and make the necessary compromises for a good relationship.

"It's very important to be flexible," she said. "One friend, a widow who claims she wants to remarry, once told me, 'I could never share my home or my bed.' How could she expect to marry again with that attitude? If you don't bend, you break. That's good advice at any age."

MADDIE
Be proactive

Maddie, widowed after a forty-year marriage and five children, didn't think she'd ever remarry. But marry she did, at 68, to a widower with eight children. They met through mutual friends. Together they have 15 grandchildren. She's one of the sexy grandmas you met in Chapter 3.

"Learn to be alone and independent before you even think of marrying again," she said. "For those of us who married in the '50s, it's too easy to fall back into those old patterns of expecting men to take care of us. Become an independent woman, be self-reliant, interested in life. Travel, study, make friends with dynamic single women, keep your married friends.

"I didn't think I'd ever marry again because I believed the statistics. I was sure there was no one out there for me. But I wasn't concerned, because I liked the single life, especially the fact that I was not accountable to anyone but myself," she said. "I had learned to overcome loneliness, and I enjoyed many interests, alone or with friends."

Maddie said she was single for six years before her remarriage. During that time she made many different types of friends for sharing the different areas of her life—some for the ballet, some for travel, others for theater or museums.

"Bring people into your life, don't wait for them to call you," she said. "I did it through having dinner parties or inviting someone to see a movie with me, but I didn't do these things to meet men, I did them because I thoroughly enjoy these activities and in the doing, I met interesting people and made wonderful, lifelong friends of both sexes."

BERNICE
First, know thyself

Bernice lost her second husband in an auto accident when she was in her early 30s. She was left with a set of twins, barely three years old, from that marriage, and two teenage boys from her first marriage, which had ended in divorce. She was definitely not a merry widow. Her previous two husbands were abusive alcoholics and she vowed never to make that mistake again. When she did remarry ten years later, she picked a much younger man than herself. She was 44 and Walter was 26.

"Walter was and is my second son's best friend," she said. "Our relationship developed over time into one of love. Before we married, we had known each other for about eight or nine years, but we didn't even begin to become friends until about three years before we married. To this day, we are each other's best friend and this, I believe, is the highest prerequisite to love."

Bernice believes strongly that before you can find the right man, you have to find out who you are.

"Stop outer-focusing, and start inner-focusing," she said. "When my second husband died, I was left with four kids to raise on my own. I had no time for socializing or going out to meet men. All I had time for was working in a grocery store, raising my kids and trying to figure out how to get out of the financial mess I was in. I had no money, I had nothing. I lived in a crummy neighborhood and constantly worried about my sons getting in with the wrong crowd. I couldn't go out at night because I couldn't afford baby sitters."

But she did make time for two important activities that helped her get through it—keeping a daily journal of her thoughts and reading self-help books.

"Keeping a journal was one of the best things I ever did for myself," she said. "Every evening I wrote down anything that came to mind. What I was feeling, what I was thinking, what I was doing. Anything and everything. Sometimes I'd write pages and pages. It helped me see the things that were screwing me up. I think that was the biggest help of all. I also made up my mind that life *was* going to get better and I was going to make it better.

"I'm a big reader, always have been," she continued. "I've read millions of books in my lifetime. I can't say it was one particular book that turned my life around, but books definitely did help me a lot. They help you pick up a different pattern of thinking. This is true of all types of books, not just the self-help ones, although they were especially helpful."

Bernice said that through her reading and journal writing, she gained insights into why her first two husbands were so wrong for her and what she would need in a new relationship. About that time Walter entered her life, but only as her son's friend. It would be another eight years before the romance blossomed.

"Sometimes the age difference between me and Walter is a problem," she said, "but our different perspectives have helped both of us. We often see things in totally different ways. When that happens, he tries to figure out how I feel and I try to figure out how he sees things. It's more of a challenge than I expected, but we work through it.

"I'm happier in this marriage than I ever was in my other two. We don't fight all the time. We try to work out our problems without fighting, something that never happened with my other husbands," she said.

Unlike some of the women who think older men make better husbands, Bernice thinks marrying a younger man is definitely the way to go.

"Men in their 20s and 30s are much more tuned in to how women think," she said. "Walter's generation is different from men of my generation. A younger man is more inclined to listen to what a woman is thinking. Older men are more set in their ways, some of them are very old-fashioned in their thinking. Everything is either this way or that way. They look at you funny if you try to get them to see something in a different light. It's as if they figured it all out when they were younger, decided that's the way things ought to be, and then forgot about the reasons why."

To Be or Not to Be—Live-in Lovers First?

Sixty-one of the Marriage 100 lived with their husbands before marrying them—some for a few months, others for several years. For a lot of the women, living with a man first is a must. One said it should be mandatory. Six were totally against it for religious or moral reasons, others said it's OK if you don't have children at home. But seven did have children at home when they decided to live with their future husbands and things worked out just fine.

Do you think you should test the waters first? Or are you against it? Let's see how some of the Marriage 100 feel about this.

EMILY

It should be mandatory

"It should be mandatory. It's a way to find out if you can work with each other," said Emily, who lived with David for two years before they wed. "I had severe doubts about getting married again, so we decided to live together first. But I wasn't taking any chances—I left everything in boxes when I moved out of my house and into his, just in case."

MADDIE

Do it!

"Fred and I only lived together for a month before we were married, which is too short a time," said Maddie, the widow who remarried at 68. "I think you should probably live together longer than we did because the longer you live together, the better you know each other and the easier it is to resolve differences *before* you marry.

"For us, living together for even a month was helpful," she continued. "We learned a lot about each other in that short time, things it might have taken months to learn otherwise."

JUNE AND RITA

It's wrong

Not surprisingly, those who were against a couple's living together before marriage were mostly those with strong religious convictions.

"I don't think it's the right thing to do," said June, who met her second husband at a church function and is deeply involved with church activities.

Rita added, "It is wrong, according to God's word." She met her second husband in the church choir, and their first date was attending church together the following Sunday.

Jean and Vivian
It depends

For the majority of the women, personal circumstances were the deciding factor.

"I didn't live with my husband before marriage, but I have no moral objections to it," said Jean. "It depends on your circumstances. If you have children at home, I'm against it. But otherwise, it's your business."

Vivian added, "I think it really depends on the two people involved, but I don't think a live-in relationship should be rushed into because emotionally it's sometimes just as hard to end a live-in relationship as it is to end a marriage. " Vivian lived with her husband, Ray, for one year before they wed.

Olivia and Billie
It's a must

"We lived together for a year before getting married," said Olivia. "For Herb and me it was extremely important, since neither of us had been married before and we were both nervous about whether we could adjust to living with someone. For me, it took a lot of the fear out of getting married."

Billie, who agrees, said, "I think it's extremely important to live together because you find out a great deal about each other by being together day to day—juggling schedules and dealing with the nitty gritty of responsibilities." She lived with Ben for ten months before marrying him.

ROBERTA
Don't, he might not marry you

Roberta doesn't think it's immoral for a couple to live together before marriage, but she questions whether it's wise, since the man might be perfectly content with the status quo and be in no hurry to marry.

"I didn't want to move in with Ted before we were married because it takes him a long time to make decisions," said Roberta. "I figured our marriage might be put off for years if we lived together. As it was, it took him more than twenty years to decide to marry in the first place and two years to make up his mind to marry me." Roberta was 41 and Ted 49 when they wed, both for the first time.

KATHLEEN
Yes, it eases tension

"Both of us had been single for a long time following our divorces and we were both afraid of getting married again," said Kathleen. "Living together for a few months helped a lot, and when we did marry, there was no tension. I thought I'd seen all his bad habits during that time—but he managed to keep a couple hidden until we were married."

JOANNA
It's OK, but legally risky

"Ernest and I lived together for six months before we were married," said Joanna. "We knew that we could easily live together for the rest of our lives without marriage. But marriage afforded our union the dignity that living together doesn't always achieve. Legally, living together is riskier. You have many more rights as a spouse. Our biggest fear was that if (God forbid) one of us became seriously ill, we might not be allowed to be by each other's side or make life and death decisions for each other. The law supports the legal spouse on this, but not necessarily the live-in companion. It's murky in most states when it comes to the rights of lovers. I wouldn't want to take any chances."

Chris
It could be better than marriage

Chris has an opposite point of view: "I think living together is a great idea. In fact, given the various legal and financial complications of divorce and remarriage, it may be a desirable alternative for those who are beyond the age of wanting to start a family."

Hilda, Sandra, and Maureen
Not with kids at home

Many said that living together before marriage is a good idea, but only if there are no children at home. Hilda, Sandra, and Maureen all concur.

"It's fine if your kids are grown," said Hilda, who wed for the third time at 54 and lived with her husband for one month before marrying him. "If you have dependents, think twice, because it doesn't set a good example. If you're alone, I think it's just fine."

"I have nothing against it and think it's fine if that's what you want. However, when I was married in the early '70s, it was not as easily accepted by society as it is now," said Sandra. "I had an unmarried daughter in her 20s at the time I met Joseph and even though she wasn't living at home, I felt I should set a good example for her. Today it's not such a big deal, but I still think you should think twice if you have children, even grown ones, still living with you."

"I see no problem if there are no children at home, but I am very much against it if children are involved. It sends the wrong moral message," said Maureen, who married for the first time at 41 and lived with her husband for a year before marrying him. "However, if you don't have kids at home, I would encourage it so you don't become too set in your ways. Also, it's good to know in advance what you're getting into."

Once again we see that there are many different viewpoints on virtually every topic concerning marriage and relationships. But the one common thread is take your time and get to know him well.

Listen Up

Don't rush into it! Those four words were expressed by virtually all of the women. Most of them dated their future husbands for a year or two before marrying them, and the majority lived with them for at least a few months. And as for those who've been there, one divorcee, who rewed at 42, had this piece of advice, "Remember everything you disliked about your first marriage and make sure your 'intended' isn't going to give you a repeat performance."

Remember, too, that you're not alone if you suddenly find you're afraid to take a chance on a guy, or you feel frightened when your longed-for dreams of marriage start to materialize. Most of the women will tell you to listen and trust that inner voice that says "yes" or "no." Here are a few more words of wisdom from the Marriage 100:

Don't let the jitters scare you off. Anxiety attacks, nervousness, and second thoughts are normal when you make major changes in your life, and nothing is more major than marriage. The jitters, if any, are temporary, and there are lots of resources to see you through them. Follow the lead of many of these women—talk to friends or counselors, take self-help courses, read self-help books, try meditating. These are all good ways for calming your fears and seeing things in a better light. When something is troubling me, I take a brisk walk in Central Park with my dog and talk to her as we walk—she never fails me. By the end of the walk,

I've usually gathered some new insights, not to mention some amused looks.

Take a chance. While we can all learn from experience, so many women are afraid to take a chance on a new man because they get caught up in the past and are afraid of making the same mistakes again. "I was a little bit afraid of marriage because I remember how my first marriage restricted me and I didn't want that again," said Linda, who married for the second time at 48. "When I divorced my husband after twenty-three years, I just wanted to be free. I didn't want to have anyone telling me what to do. I needed to do stuff for myself and I wanted to continue working. I wanted to ski, play tennis, do all the things for myself that I enjoyed, without having to listen to complaints." Guess what. She found a man who wanted that for her, too. She didn't have to give up doing the things she really loves.

Keep your eyes and ears open. Get to know him and his family. Observe how he treats those around him. Most of the women agreed that you're not ready for marriage to a particular man until you've looked at all the facts. "Gather all the information you can on him, before making a decision," said one, who wed for the first time at 49. "Know his financial situation, his relationship with his children and his ex-wife (if any), his parents, his co-workers, his neighbors. If you observe a lot of negatives, beware."

Marriage is not a cure-all. Don't look for marriage to solve your problems, was another central idea. "If you are unhappy, marriage is not going to make you happy," said a divorcee who remarried at 41. "Before you even think of marriage, you must be comfortable with yourself and be a responsible adult. Do not look to be rescued or taken care of." Another, who wed for the second time at 45, said, "Before you leap into a marriage, ask yourself, 'Why?' Make sure you're not trying to be rescued from an unhappy or boring life. And don't rush into another relationship after a divorce or breakup of a long relationship. *Feel* all your feelings and decide what went wrong with the previous relationships, without assigning blame. If necessary, get counseling or join a support group." Another, who wed for the third time at 48, said, "Men who are worth the effort don't want someone who is too needy, emotionally or financially. Neither should you."

Don't expect perfection. No one is perfect, as anyone who's been married knows only too well. "You must be ready to close your eyes to imperfections," said one woman who wed for the first time at 49. "You're not perfect and neither is he, so accept what you can't change."

So, the bottom line is, stay cool, chill out, don't panic. Good advice for any situation, but especially helpful when you're trying to figure out where to meet someone who will eventually change your life. The good news is that they're out there. In the next chapter, we'll find out how some of the Marriage 100 met their husbands and spotlight some of the organizations that helped them meet men.

Chapter 5

Where the Guys Are

If there are no fish in this place, drop your hook in another.

—Chinese proverb

There's obviously no one way to meet men. For every woman who met a so-called loser at a singles party, there's one who met a winner. For every woman who hates the bar scene, there's one who thinks bars are great places to meet men. Some said you must work at meeting men, others said the best way to find is not to look.

Judging from how the Marriage 100 met their husbands, the best way to meet men is still the old-fashioned way—through friends and relatives or through work: 35 of the women met their husbands on blind dates, at parties, or through introductions, all arranged by friends or relatives, and 27 met their husbands through work (five married the boss). Of the rest (and you've already met some of them), 13 met their husbands through singles organizations, personal ads, and dating services; 9, while participating in sports; 7, through church related activities; 6, pursuing special interests; 2, in a bar; 2 wed their physicians; 1 met her second husband at her first husband's funeral; another met her husband on a commuter train, and yet another in an elevator. One woman, a widow in her 60s, took matters into her own hands and started a singles group at work, "How not to be lonely," and that's where she met her second husband. You just never know.

Blind Dates, Friends, and Relatives

Every one of the women who met her husband on a blind date (and there were eight of them), agreed to the date reluctantly. Yet all were happily surprised and now are the first to encourage other women to take a chance if friends or relatives say, "Have I got a great guy for you!" Don't ignore your grown children, either, if they say they know someone you might like—three of the women met their husbands through their children (and one through her future husband's daughter). About a dozen others were introduced through friends at parties and weddings.

EMILY
Take a doberman—just in case

One of those who agreed to a blind date with extreme reluctance, and got lucky, was Emily, the twice-divorced grandmother. She's the one you met earlier who thinks "dating sucks."

It happened when a girlfriend of Emily's, who was twelve years her junior, insisted on setting her up on a blind date. The lucky guy was David, a good friend of the young woman's 50-something boyfriend.

"I had been divorced and living alone for ten years and I liked it that way," said Emily. "I really didn't want to go on any type of date, blind or otherwise, because getting involved with a man again was the last thing on my mind. I made some pretty bad choices with men in the past and I wasn't ready to try again. And, frankly, I was terrified of the idea—I was a grandmother, for God's sake.

"My friend kept insisting and finally I gave in," she continued. "She lived fifty miles away and suggested I spend the weekend at her place. I said OK, but I took my doberman with me, just in case

I needed an excuse for a fast exit. My friend was in her early 30s, so I was expecting my date to be about her age, and I was sure he was expecting a babe, someone young, blond, and beautiful like her.

"While I was waiting at her house to meet David, a guy who was a friend of hers walked in, roaring drunk," she continued. "He picked me up and swirled me around and I thought, 'I'm outta here.' My friend ushered him out—thank God, that wasn't my date, after all. But David was late. Now I'm thinking, 'Hmmm, this is not going well' and trying to find an excuse to leave. Then David walked in and I fell into his eyes. They are hazel and very expressive and I've never forgotten that moment.

"I was so relieved to find that David was a mature man, in his late 50s and also a grandparent. The four of us went out for dinner and dancing, and David and I were so involved in our conversations with each other that the other two no longer existed. Afterward, David invited me to his place for bacon and eggs. It was 3:00 A.M. and very romantic—until I remembered the dog."

Before they sat down for breakfast, she had put the dog in David's garage: "The dog had terrible diarrhea and made a total mess of the garage," she said. "It was not exactly the perfect ending to a wonderful night." But it didn't dampen their enthusiasm for each other. They moved in together almost immediately and were married three years after that blind date (and after she found a new home for her dog).

Arlene

Listen to your daughter

Arlene, the divorced mother of five grown children whom you met in Chapter 4, said she had no interest in dating anyone when she met Jim on a blind date. Both were in their 50s.

"I was involved with foster children, as well as my own kids and grandchildren," she said. "I also was very involved with my church and was a member of two community choral groups. Life was good, I was content. Dating was the last thing on my mind."

That all changed when one of her daughters, who knew Jim from work, insisted Arlene meet him. She was convinced they were right for each other and pressed for them to meet.

"It was a double date, with my daughter and her boyfriend," said Arlene. "Susan and her date picked me up and we drove forty-five miles to a very nice restaurant. Jim lived fifty miles from the restaurant in the opposite direction. When I met Jim, my immediate reaction was that he was a pleasant enough person, but I didn't feel any great chemistry between us and I assumed he didn't either. I thought that any future contact would be very unlikely, but I might as well enjoy a nice dinner—and I did."

To her surprise, Jim called a few weeks later for another dinner date, this time just the two of them. And this time they clicked. One thing they found out they both had in common was their love of children, not just their own twelve from previous marriages, but also the dozens of foster children Arlene's helped through the years who stay in touch.

RONNIE
Forget "He's not your type"

Usually it's single men who are invited by hostesses to help fill a dinner table. But in Ronnie's case, she was the one who was invited "just to even up" the number at the table. She was seated next to Ken, a single man who the hostess was certain was not her type.

"She told me she didn't think I would be the least bit interested in him, which made me wonder why she sat us together. Looking back on it, I often think that maybe she just said that so I wouldn't be uptight about it," said Ronnie, a research biologist who was in her early 40s and never married when she met Ken.

"I liked him immediately," she continued. "He was quiet and shy, but very pleasant and we really enjoyed talking to each other over dinner. I felt safe with him, that it was OK for me to express myself and show my vulnerable side."

Ken called her the next day and, because she was new to the area, took her on a long drive along the coast north of San Francisco.

"Within the first two to three months of dating, we both knew that we belonged together," she said.

Ronnie said she was definitely interested in finding a husband when she met Ken and once even joined a dating service, an experience she believes helped make her more relaxed about meeting men.

"I wanted to be married for a long time, to share my life with someone, belong to a family, feel loved. But I was the shy type and didn't date much," she said. "I was in my late 30s when I joined a dating service. I met lots of nice men, and although none panned out as marriage partners, I believe the experience of the dating service prepared me to meet Ken. In my opinion, no experience in life is ever wasted, and the dating service was a good example of that."

FAY
Make your own choices

Fay is another example of how friends, no matter how well meaning, are not always the best judges of who is or is not right for someone. Like Ronnie's hostess, Fay's friend was dead wrong about the type of man she'd fall for.

"I met Ron when a mutual friend invited us both over for dinner, but there was a caveat," she said. "My friend informed me, 'This invitation is not to fix you up. He is not your type.' She honestly did not think we'd be compatible and was very surprised to find we started seeing each other right away."

You can't blame the hostess. Fay, if you'll recall, is the one who said she and her husband have virtually no shared interests.

They were married a year after that dinner party. Fay was 45, Ron was 53, each divorced with two adult children.

"I was definitely in the market for a new commitment when I met Ron," she said. "I had been divorced for two years, following a twenty-four-year, unhappy marriage. I wanted to have a loving relationship, which I felt deprived of in my first marriage. Ron is very different from my first husband. He's close to his feelings and expresses them easily—that's one of the reasons I was attracted to him. Also, he wants to please me and will not make major decisions without discussing them with me—qualities that were lacking in my first husband."

Caroline

Don't give up!

Caroline, the divorcee with four grown children whose advice (in Chapter 3) was, "Get a life," met her husband through his daughter.

"His daughter told me she thought her father, a widower, and I might like each other and asked if she could give him my phone number. I figured, why not?"

He called, they went out to dinner three days later, were inseparable after that, and got married one year later.

"My friends were thrilled," said Caroline. "I became a source of hope and inspiration, an example of good things that can happen to a woman later in life. Don't give up! You just never know what life (and your friends) has to offer."

Joyce

Beware the jealous "friend"

Although Joyce also met her second husband, Ken, through a friend, the friend wasn't very happy about how well they hit it off.

"Ken was a widower whom a married friend of mine was trying to introduce to 'appropriate' women," she said. "One weekend she invited me to her summer home on Cape Cod as part of a plot she hatched to break up a possible romance between Ken and a neighbor. She didn't think the neighbor was 'appropriate' for Ken. She was certain he wouldn't be interested in me, so she felt it was safe for me to be there as a decoy. Matchmaking was the last thing on her mind.

"When I walked through the door and laid eyes on Ken, I felt truly struck by lightning," she continued. "He forgot all about the neighbor who was after him, and we spent the weekend taking long walks on the beach together, talking nonstop. My hostess was thrilled because he had apparently forgotten about the neighbor. That is, she was thrilled until she found out a month later that Ken and I were dating.

"She tried to dissuade me; at one point she said, 'You're nothing like his late wife—she was so intelligent, so thin, so elegant—not at all like you.' How's that for a friend?"

It didn't work. They were married six months later; Joyce was 50, Ken was 67.

"There are lots of wonderful men out there. If someone wants to play matchmaker and introduce you to a friend, take the risk," she said. "It's a terrific opportunity to fall in love and have an exciting, romantic life. Don't let age, a few extra pounds, or so-called friends discourage you."

Rita
Don't be embarrassed

Rita said she almost died when a friend asked a male acquaintance if he knew of any good men for her.

"I was divorced with a daughter in her late teens and had just moved to Albuquerque. A friend I met through church invited me to go shopping with her one afternoon," said Rita. "As we were driving home, she pulled into a nursery owned by a friend of hers. We stopped to say hello and her friend, George, gave us a tour of the nursery and a small plant as a gift. As we were leaving, my friend said, 'Oh, by the way, George, would you happen to know a nice man for my lady friend?' I was horribly embarrassed, mortified. But he wrote down my name and phone number and, to my great surprise, he called a month later to tell me he had found a man for me, a newly divorced friend of his wife's.

"George and his wife invited me to their mobile home park for a formal dinner dance," she said. "That's where they introduced me to Larry. I was very impressed with his intelligence and his gentle manner." They were married three months later, both for the second time. She was 46, he was 40.

Meeting Men Through Work

One of the major advantages in meeting someone through work is that you probably already know him pretty well, and if you don't, it's easy enough to ask around—discreetly, of course. It doesn't take long to know if he is a workaholic or an alcoholic, whether he's honest, thoughtful, outgoing, or shy and, most importantly, how he treats others. As one woman said, "My future husband was highly respected by those he supervised; he tried to bring out the best in people. I was very impressed with those qualities because I thought it was a good indication of how he would treat me and my children after we were married. And I wasn't wrong."

Most of the women who met their husbands through work said they had known them for years but had never considered them as potential marriage partners. Sometimes, you tend to ignore what's right under your nose. As one said, "Look around, you never know . . ."

They Married the Boss

Who says office romances don't work—five of the Marriage 100 married the boss. Three of them we met earlier: Annette, the secretary who quit work to write a book; Pat, the marketing executive who was loaned out to her future husband; and Judy, a school counselor who wed the district superintendent. Joining the group is Susan, an office manager, who wed the executive who hired her for his department, and Cassie, a single mother and administrative assistant who worked for what she initially thought was a "very boring accountant type."

SUSAN

Don't listen to malcontents

Susan was working at a pharmaceutical company as a temp when she met Len. He was a quality controls manager, and when he found out that her temporary assignment was ending, he requested that she be hired as an office manager for his department.

"We worked together for six months in tight quarters and became very good friends," she said. "I found myself falling in love with him, but I tried not to show it. What I didn't realize was that he had fallen in love with me long before I went to work for him, which is why he wanted me in his department. He never let on how he felt, which was good, because it allowed me to be myself," she said. "When I first started working for Len, I was in a relationship that wasn't going well and ended shortly after that," she continued. "I was frustrated and confused, and started confiding in him and a strong bond developed between us that ultimately led to love.

"My initial reaction to him was negative because a woman in the company told me he was power hungry, and I had been swayed by her opinion," she said. "After I started working for him, I realized she was dead wrong. He was a gentle person with a great sense of humor."

After a few months, her job was eliminated and she was let go, which turned out to be a blessing in disguise.

"We didn't start dating until I lost my job," she said. "I guess we were both shy about getting involved while we worked together. The last day of my employment, when we knew we wouldn't be seeing each other at work anymore, we sort of admitted we had feelings for each other. We exchanged phone numbers and he called me two days later. I went to his house for wine and cheese and then out to dinner. He told me he fell in love with me shortly after we met and he knew he would marry me. I never had a clue he felt that way." They were married two months later. She was 40, he was 47. It was her third marriage, his second. Neither has children.

Cassie

He doesn't have to be Jewish

"Steve was single—a widower with three grown daughters—when I started working for him. I wasn't the least bit interested in him romantically. I thought he was boring, very dry, a typical accountant," she said. "I'd been working for him for about a year and a half when he asked me to have a drink with him after work. It was very casual, but that evening I saw a different side of him. All I could think was, 'If only he were Jewish.'"

Thanks to advice from her mother, Cassie decided to put aside her feelings about marrying outside her faith.

"I had always said that I would never marry someone who wasn't Jewish," she continued. "But mother knows best—she always said, 'Don't close the door on anyone until you get to know him.'"

Steve, it turns out, had his own prerequisites, and they had to do with age, not religion.

"I found out that the day after our first drink together, he checked to see how old I was because he promised his daughters that he wouldn't bring home anybody younger than they were," she said. "As long as I was older, he would consider dating me. So you see, being young isn't always such an advantage." When they wed, Cassie was 47 (15 years older than the oldest daughter) and Steve, 59.

Through Work, Sort Of...

Several of the women didn't actually work with their future husbands, but met them through work-related activities. One met her husband at a media event; another, when she switched from coffee breaks to "Bible breaks," and a third, while she was tending bar.

FRAN
Ignore the toupee

Fran, a New York writer and artist, who wed for the second time at 45, was covering a weekend media event at Disney World in Orlando when she met Craig, a 37-year-old bachelor and fellow writer from New York.

"The invitation was for two, but I didn't have anyone to invite so I went alone," she said. "It was practically all couples and I really felt like a third wheel. I hung out with an editor friend of mine and her boyfriend, but I felt really dorky. I thought, 'I'm the only person here without a significant other.' Then I relaxed and decided to just do my thing and have a good time. My biggest hang-up on being by myself was going on the rides alone."

She met Craig when she happened to sit next to him at an afternoon news conference.

"He started talking to me, but I didn't give it much thought because I assumed he was with someone; after all, everyone else was," she said. "Then I thought, 'What the hell, talk to the guy.' So I said, 'I assume you're here with your family' and he said, 'No, I'm alone.' All I could think was, 'Oh boy, here's someone to go on rides with.'"

Little did she know she was about to become a research subject for a book Craig was writing on the joy of baldness.

"Craig was wearing a toupee, which was obvious to me, but I guess he thought it looked natural," she continued. "He was testing his theory that women react differently to men with hair. I didn't know that at the time and wouldn't find out until our first date back in New York.

"We were the only unattached people at the party, so we stuck together for the rest of the weekend, going on the rides together and sitting together at meals. There was something weird about him—but I couldn't put my finger on it. What I didn't know was that he was nervous about having this hairpiece on his head and wasn't being himself. I wasn't getting the real (bald) Craig, but I wasn't paying much attention, to me he was just an escort for the weekend." Stay tuned to find out what happens when Craig flips his wig (Chapter 6).

CHERYL

Try Bible breaks

Instead of coffee and lunch breaks, Cheryl, Peter, and several other employees had "Bible Breaks" at the pharmaceutical company where they worked. She was a lab technician and he was a chemist.

"A bunch of us decided to study the Bible together during our free time, and that's how I got to know Peter," she said. "We worked in different departments, so we hadn't met until then.

"At the time, I was separated from my first husband, but still legally married to him. I never dreamed Peter would someday be my husband. I thought I was married for life to my first husband, even though we no longer lived together. When I met Peter, I just felt a lot of spiritual energy and knew a lot of prayers were going up and being answered whenever we were in the same room together."

A few months later she filed for divorce, and then moved in with Peter for two years while her divorce was being finalized.

"My mom told me we were going straight to hell—but we felt we were married in God's eyes from the first night we spent together," she said.

They were married in 1995. She was 52, and the mother of three, he was 48, and the father two. It was the second marriage for both of them. Except for her mother, everyone was happy for them.

To single women, she says, "Follow your heart. I did, and I haven't regretted this marriage for one minute."

RUBY

Doing dinner works better than lunch

Ruby was 65 and George, 63 when they wed, both for the first time. They were high school teachers who had worked together for twenty-two years and did lunch together for fifteen of those years.

"We had lunch together in the school cafeteria almost every day for fifteen years," she said. "We were good friends, but never dated each other. I don't know why, it just never occurred to either one of us. We both dated others. I was too involved in my work to think about marriage. Also, I swore I would never marry a teacher—I guess that's why I never thought of George as anything but a good friend. In my younger days I wanted someone who made a lot of money and that definitely did not include teachers."

It wasn't until Ruby retired that George asked her for a real date—dinner to celebrate her retirement. They were married ten months later.

"It's funny, but after fifteen years of having lunch together, we fell in love on our first dinner date and knew within a week that we would marry," she said. "The qualities that attracted me were qualities he'd always had—he's kind, really nice to others, very presentable, and flexible."

She doesn't think finding a husband when you're over 40, or even 50 or 60, is difficult.

"Many of my friends were well over 40 when they married. What's important is to get involved and stay involved in activities you genuinely enjoy. I met loads of candidates for marriage through boating and golfing, two activities I took up in my 60s," she said. "It's ironic that I ended up marrying someone who'd been in my life all those years."

Ruby's experience just goes to show that the grass is not always greener on the other side. Look around—your future husband may be closer than you think.

DEBBIE

First, be happy with yourself

Debbie, a bartender, met her husband, a Navy officer, at the restaurant where she worked.

"John came in one evening with a regular customer who was a good friend of his," she said. "I found John very attractive and considerate and I felt he was someone I could have an honest conversation with.

"I usually didn't pay much attention to the men who came to the bar, other than to serve them drinks," she continued. "I had one bad marriage and several co-dependent relationships behind me, and was too tired to work on a new relationship. When John came into my life, I had been single for fourteen years."

They had their first date four months later and were wed two years later, after living together for over a year. She was 42, he was 45.

As for the view that a woman over 35 is more likely to be kidnapped by terrorists than to find a husband, Debbie says, "What a crock. You'll find a husband, if that's what you really want. But first, be happy and content with yourself, be able to support yourself and be open to change. And keep your eyes open—you just never know where he's going to turn up."

The Bar Scene

Two of the women met their husbands in a bar (other than Debbie the bartender). You met one earlier, Dottie, the stockbroker who met her husband in a bar in Maine. The other woman, Sandy, met her husband at a hotel bar on Fire Island on a rainy Fourth of July weekend.

"It was one of those miserable weekends at the beach where all it did was rain and everyone was grumpy," said Sandy. "There wasn't much to do, so two friends and I went to a local bar for a drink. Bill saw us come in and came over to our table and struck up a conversation with us. At first, I didn't like him. I thought he was too aggressive, and I usually don't like men assuming they can join a tableful of women."

She gave him her phone number, anyway, and three days later she went out to dinner with him. About a month later they decided to marry. It was the second marriage for both. She was 47 and he was 49.

More on the Bar Scene

While only two women out of a hundred met their husband in a bar, many more said they frequented bars when they were single and thought it could be a perfectly fine place to meet men—provided you follow a few basic rules. Here is what some had to say about the bar scene:

- Don't go to bars that are known pickup places, go to quality places where people stop by after work.
- Go early, right after work—and leave before 7:00 P.M., because after that the heavy drinkers take over.
- If you want to meet men, don't go to bars with a group of women (or anywhere else, for that matter). Go with one friend, and leave with that friend.
- If someone asks for your number, ask for his instead. Try to get his home phone and his business card; if he won't give them to you, forget him.

Singles Organizations

A lot of people like to put them down, but the fact remains: single groups are still a good way to meet men.

ELISE
Follow your interests

Elise is a perfect example of, "Do what interests you, but keep your antennae out." A travel writer in her 50s, she wrote a newspaper article about the Travel Companion Exchange (TCE) and was so impressed by the group that she decided to join and see if she could find a fellow (male) traveler. She not only found someone fun to travel with, she also found another travel writer and a widower, whom she eventually married. A divorced mother of three and a grandmother, Elise had been single for fifteen years before she met Jeff through TCE. She was 52 when they wed.

"I wanted to remarry. I thought it would be lovely to find someone to share my life with," she said. "When you're on the road a lot, as I am, it's hard to meet men. I thought TCE would be a good way to combine meeting men with my love of travel."

Travel Companion Exchange is for singles who want to find travel companions, usually of the opposite sex. The majority of its members are over 40. You fill out a profile checklist and answer questions, such as, "Do you like adventure travel, nightlife, museums? Is your travel budget limited? Given the right person, would you like an intimate friendship? A coded personal ad is listed in the TCE bimonthly newsletter, from which members can request profiles and photos.

"I met about three dozen guys through my ad, and I traveled with about 12 of them, on a platonic basis," said Elise. "They were all very nice. What TCE does is put you in contact with someone who has the same travel interests. You set up your own schedule.

"When Jeff saw my ad, he wrote me immediately because he was thrilled to find another travel writer," she continued. "We sent each other copies of some of our published articles. I was really impressed by his writing and he was impressed by mine—that meant a lot to both of us."

They talked on the phone a few times and then met for lunch in New York City, where she lived. He came down from a small town near Albany, about three hours north of the city.

"I thought he was a lovely man, but I didn't have a strong physical attraction to him at first—that grew with love, when I realized we were on the same wavelength," she said. Three weeks after their first lunch, he invited her to spend a weekend in his home.

"I went up on a Friday, and we had a great time roaming around town the next day," she said. "I had my own room. He was a perfect gentlemen, no pushy advances. That weekend I began to see the possibilities of a serious relationship. We were so easy with each other, we could talk about anything. He's a great listener and so am I, probably because we're both writers. I thought that here was a truly sensitive, lovely guy who was also funny, interesting, and sexy. I began to realize that I was falling in love with him."

What also impressed her was a spiritual quality about him: "That first weekend he invited me to join a meditation group he led on Sundays. I stayed and was very touched by what I saw—a spiritual quality in him that I'd never seen in a man before."

Jeff, who writes a lot about train travel, invited Elise to join him on a luxury train ride through Switzerland. Elise said yes, but first, she had to spend six weeks in London, where her married son lives, helping baby-sit her only grandchild, a commitment she'd made months earlier.

"I'd forgotten how difficult and exhausting infants can be," she said. "But Jeff helped keep my spirits up by calling me every day and sending me funny little notes. Thanks to him, taking care of an infant again didn't seem quite so awful."

Jeff went to London at the end of the six weeks and met her son and daughter-in-law before whisking Elise off to Switzerland for their train trip together. They both liked him immediately.

"My daughter-in-law said, 'He's just the perfect guy for you.' Later, when my two other children met him, they had the same reaction. Jeff is very easy-going, just the opposite of their father, who is a Type A—always high-powered and pressured."

Jeff proposed during the train ride through Switzerland, but Elise wasn't sure she was ready, and jokingly told him she wouldn't marry anyone who couldn't afford to give her a diamond the size of a turnip.

"A few weeks later, back home, he presented me with a large Tiffany's box with a big blue ribbon," she said. "Inside, was a turnip with a note, 'Marry me and I'll give you diamonds the size of turnips.' This time I said yes. I didn't get a diamond quite that large, but we did go shopping together right after that and picked out a beautiful diamond ring that's just right." They were married two months later. More about that and their bubble-blowing bridesmaids in Chapter 7.

Check it out: Travel Companion Exchange, founded in 1982, publishes a bimonthly newsletter with some 500 listings, mostly of people over 40, plus tips for travel-minded singles. Contact them at P.O. Box 833, Amityville, NY 11701, 516-454-0880 or 800-392-1256 (USA only), or visit their website, http://www.whytravelalone.com.

PAULA AND JULIE
Try Parents Without Partners

Four of the women met their husbands at Parents Without Partners (PWP). One is Paula, mother of two, who rewed at 41. "I had been divorced for four months, after a fourteen-year marriage, and I decided I was ready to try again," she said. "I only dated men who were potential marriage partners and I felt this was a good organization for meeting such men. I went to their events for six weeks before I met Mike."

Another was Julie, divorced mother of two teenagers, who met Tim at PWP and married him seven months later when she was 41. "I was definitely looking. I had been single for two years and missed the companionship of a male. My kids were delighted when I remarried and welcomed Jim into the family with lots of enthusiasm."

Check it out: Parents Without Partners, founded in 1957, has 63,000 members in the USA and Canada. According to its literature, it is 55 percent female, 45 percent male, with ages ranging from 18 to 80. Most members have teenage children. Contact them at 401 N. Michigan Ave., Chicago, IL 60611-4267; 312-644-6610, or visit their website, http://www.parentswithoutpartners.org.

Barbara
Try Single Booklovers

Remember Barbara (Chapter 2) who met her husband through Single Booklovers? In the next chapter you'll hear more about what happens when Barbara and her husband finally decide to meet face-to-face after three months of letter writing. In the meantime . . .

Check it out: Single Booklovers, founded in 1970, publishes a monthly newsletter with member profiles, plus member-written book reviews and other items of interest to people who like to read. Contact them at Box 117, Gradyville PA 19039; 610-358-5049, or through their e-mail, SBL@compuserve.com.

Olivia and Iris
Try dating services

Although about a dozen of the Marriage 100 tried a dating service and most thought it was a good way to meet men, only two actually met their husbands that way. Both are women you met in Chapter 3. One, Olivia, met her husband through a Jewish dating service in New York City (the first marriage for both of them). Another, Iris, joined a service in San Diego and met her third husband: "He joined a Jewish dating service and didn't meet anyone he liked. Then he joined a nondenominational service and met me, a Quaker."

Olivia, who was 43 when she wed Herb, said she decided to try a dating service to start circulating again after ending a five-year relationship.

"I enjoyed my single life," she said. "I enjoyed my career, I had many friends and had done many wonderful things, but in a deeper sense I was lonely and anxious to pair up with someone. I yearned for a home and family."

Through the dating service they were given each other's phone numbers. They talked on the phone a few times, and met ten days later.

"My initial reaction was that he was a nice man, but not for me," she said. "But he kept calling and as I got to know him better, I realized that he is a really terrific guy." They were married nearly two years later and now have a six-year-old son.

Iris and Michael were married eight months after they met. She was 63 and marrying for the third time, he was 67 and marrying for the second time.

"I wasn't really looking for a husband," she said. "I just wanted a companion, someone to do things with. I was a widow for six years and was tired of the company of other widows."

She admits to being nervous about joining a dating service, "You're always a little nervous, filling out all those forms, wondering if you're wasting your time and money. But I think it's a good way to meet men because you state right upfront the type of man you want to meet, and you don't waste your time with someone who doesn't share your values and interests.

"My husband and I are close in age, we have the same moral values, we like the same music and we both like fishing. With a dating service you can find out things like this right away and cut to the chase," she said.

The Personals

The personals, which have been going strong since the early '70s in newspapers and magazines, now, of course, are also standard procedure on the Internet.

Jo
Working the personals

Jo, the teacher you met earlier who met her husband through the personals, has some good advice on how to "work" the personals, whether the print or on-line variety.

"First, I think you have better control if you answer ads rather than place them, but you must really *read* the ads and read between the lines," she said. "For example, I'm tall and I wanted someone over six feet, so if a guy didn't mention his height, I didn't follow up because that meant he was probably short. That holds true across the board—if he doesn't give his weight, he's probably fat, if he doesn't give his age, he's probably hiding it.

"I believe that if a man puts himself out there, is really honest about himself and what he's looking for, he is automatically saying, 'I want a relationship and I'm willing to take a chance,'" she continued. "I wouldn't answer ads that said, 'Age 50, wants 25-year-old, well-developed young lady for discreet afternoons.' But some women I know would, and they'd tell me things like, 'Well, if he's going to do that he should have an older woman.' And I would always respond, *pay attention, they mean exactly what they say*. If a guy says he doesn't want to get married, it means he doesn't want to get married; if he says he wants a busty blonde, it means he wants a busty blonde. It doesn't mean he really wants something else."

Here's what to look for in the personals, according to Jo:

- They need to say who they are—something personal about themselves. If the ad is very flowery and sentimental, that's the type of guy you're probably going to get.
- Beware if they say what they want in a woman, but say nothing about themselves. If that's the case, forget it. They must share something about themselves. Only follow up on ads by someone who says, "This is who I am, this is what I'm looking for." If they don't do both, don't answer their ad.

- If you're more comfortable placing an ad than answering one, then be very specific about yourself so you don't hear from the guys who are really looking for some other type of person. Use the same principles mentioned before in reading the letters you'll get. Whether they say it in an ad or in a letter responding to your ad, they must be specific about themselves.

Jo said she met lots of terrific guys through the personals before she met her husband.

"Before Andrew, I went out with about ten guys I met through the personals," she said. "I liked them all, except for one who was kind of boring and cheap—he took me out for a bowl of Jell-O."

She said she answered Andrew's ad because he said he was a Francophile and was looking for someone who speaks French. She, too, is a Francophile and speaks French fluently.

"We went to a French restaurant on our first date. He ordered red wine in French, or thought he did—but what he really ordered was red *wind*," she said. "I corrected him and he nearly died when he found out my French was better that his. I'm sure he was a little upset that his act was blown because he was used to really impressing the women with his French. It's a perfect example of why you should be careful what you ask for—he asked for someone who spoke French and that's what he got, only what he didn't bargain for was someone whose French was better than his.

"Andrew's ad also said he was a 'Jewnatarian,' which clinched it for me," said Jo. "That told me a lot—a Jew who is a Unitarian is, in my opinion, a searcher of truth. I'm a Unitarian and half Jewish, so I knew exactly what he was saying. Those are the kinds of clues you should look for in an ad because they tell you a lot about a man."

Lenore
Write an honest ad

Another who met her husband through the personals is Lenore, the Long Island mother of three whom you met earlier. She placed an ad in a local magazine and was honest and upfront about herself.

"When I read the ads, it seemed as if all the women said they were blond and sensual and all the men were six feet tall and wealthy," she said. "I decided to write an honest ad. I said, 'I'm 40, I'm not padded or pretentious, I don't wear a lot of makeup and I've got three kids at home. I'm looking for a decent man with a good sense of humor.'"

She said she got a "whole batch of letters from a whole batch of losers" and was about to give up, when a letter arrived from Jake.

"He only gave his phone number and when I called, a woman answered. So many men who answer these ads are married, so you can't be too careful—usually when a woman answers I hang up and don't call back. This time I didn't hang up right away and I found out the woman was his mother. After Jake and I met, I called the magazine and told them not to send me any more letters. I knew Jake was the one for me."

Madeline
Have an out

Madeline, who wed for the first time at 41, met her husband, William, through the personals, but she's keeping it a secret from her family.

"His relatives know, mine do not. They wouldn't approve," she said.

For their first encounter, she suggested they meet in a parking lot and drive separately to a restaurant, "I wasn't taking any chances, even though my first impression was very positive—I thought he was cute and fairly normal."

Cyberads

An excellent book for negotiating the personals on-line is *Men Are from Cyberspace: The Single Woman's Guide to Flirting, Dating, and Finding Love On-Line,* by Lisa Skriloff and Jodie Gould (St. Martin's Press, New York). This book will guide you through finding the best chat rooms, the best time to go on-line and what to do if you're new to the Internet. According to the authors, there are plenty of 40-plus men and women looking on-line for partners. Here's a sample Q & A from the book:

> **Q. I'm over 50 and I wasn't weaned on computers. Are there any men my age out there and will they be interested in a cybersenior?**
>
> *A. At fifty-plus, you are far from a cybersenior. And you no longer need a degree in computer science to enjoy the fruits of the Net. You and millions of other Baby Boomers are doing just that. The Big Three service providers all have chat rooms and news groups for the Baby Boomer set. AOL has a Fifty-something chat room, as well as a SeniorNet for people in their sixties and seventies. If you're divorced, there are support groups for divorcees (gay and straight). Exactly what do you have to lose by exploring for men your own age? Seek and ye shall find.*

Be Careful

Whether you're meeting someone through the personals in the print media or through the Internet, remember you are dealing with strangers, so use a little common sense:

- Do not give out your home address. Meet him in a public place and, preferably, in a group setting.
- If you're dealing with personals on-line, keep in mind that message board postings are public, so don't say anything you wouldn't want the world to know, and don't post personal information, such as your address or telephone number. You are dealing with a cyber world of strangers, and you never know who's reading your messages.

Church

Seven of the women met their husbands at church or through church-related activities. One couple, Ed and Toni, met at a church social event, when both were married to someone else.

"When Ed and I first met we got into a conversation, sat down, and three hours later we were told that the party was over. We left with our own spouses," said Toni, adding that they stayed in touch but remained with their respective spouses for another five years. "Six years later we both got divorced and married each other."

Here are a few, more typical, church-style encounters:

Rose and Jay met when they both joined the church choir. He was a widower with one son, she was divorced and mother of three. For their first date, six months later, they attended church together and afterwards went out to brunch. They were married seven months later. She was 45, he was 49.

Charlene and Luis met at a polka Mass and dance at a Catholic church. She wasn't looking for a man at the time because she was in the throes of a bitter divorce.

"I went at the urging of a friend who thought I needed to get out and have some fun," she said. "Luis came over to me and asked me to dance. I liked him right away; he seemed generous and was very talkative (he still is)." A month later they went out to eat after church. They were married five years later, after her children were grown and on their own. She was 47 and he was 49.

June and Fred, both widowed with four kids each, met in church through his daughter-in-law when Fred was visiting from another state.

"I attended the same church that his family attended and had become friends with his daughter-in-law," she said. "When Fred came to visit, they took him to church with them. His daughter-in-law introduced us at a coffee afterward, and later that evening the two of us had dinner together. I think we fell in love right then and there. A month later, I flew to his home in Florida to spend a weekend with him." After three months of a long-distance romance, they were married. She was 60, he was 59.

"I wasn't looking for a husband when I met Fred, even though I'd been alone and somewhat lonely for almost four years," she said. "I felt if God wanted me to meet someone to marry, He would put that man in my path. And He did."

Sports

At least a third of the women are actively involved in some type of sports activity and highly recommend sports as a way of meeting men—not to mention getting in shape and having fun. But only nine of the Marriage 100 actually met their future husbands through sports.

Julie is typical of the sports-minded, "The men I really enjoyed dating, I met mostly through skiing or through my tennis club. My advice is to find activities that you enjoy—if you're athletic, join gyms or sports clubs. Just keep doing what you enjoy and you'll find someone with the same interests." Not surprisingly, she met her husband on the tennis courts.

Denise and Joe: "We met on a sailboat on Cape Cod. I love sailing and was spending a week on the Cape with friends who own a boat. Joe was a neighbor of theirs who was invited along for the ride. We hit it off, had dinner together two nights later, and were married ten months later. I wasn't interested in marriage when I met

Joe. I had lots of male friends and wasn't lacking for companionship, plus I'd already been through two divorces, but Joe helped turn me around on the idea of remarriage." Denise was 59 when she wed for the third time, and Joe was 69 and marrying for the second time.

Claire and Max met hiking. "I did a lot of hiking because I loved it, not because I was trying to meet men. I went out every Sunday on group hikes with the Appalachian Mountain Club, out of New York. Max happened to be on one of the hikes and we started talking as we walked. We talked a lot and I found him pleasant, but I wasn't particularly interested in dating him or anyone else. I had one bad marriage behind me and had been single nearly twelve years. I liked being single. I saw Max on several hikes after that and eventually he asked me to have dinner with him." They were married a year after their first date, both for the second time. She was 54, he was 48.

Lola and Al met at a bowling alley. "Tell your friends and coworkers that you are available to meet eligible men, that's how I met Al," said Lola. "I belonged to a mixed bowling league that met once a week. Al was on one of the teams. Friends, who knew I was looking for someone to date, told me about him—they said he was a really nice guy and a widower. At the time, my two boys were grown and out of the house. I was lonely, and I let my friends know it. Thanks to their urging, I struck up a conversation with Al that evening. I liked him immediately. I could see he was a sincere, good man, and I was comfortable with him because I could be myself around him. He invited me out to dinner one week later and we were married a year later." She was 49, he was 65. It was her third marriage, his second.

As you can see, there are lots of different ways to meet men, and age has nothing to do with it.

I have a friend who took a class on how to flirt, at an adult education center. She's not a natural flirt and she swears the class helped her loosen up and not be afraid to make the initial contact.

One of the things she learned that works for her is to wear something interesting or unusual, such as a brooch, a hat, or a political button, when you go to a party.

"It gives people an excuse to approach you and start a conversation. And it works both ways. If you see an interesting man, look for something he's wearing or doing that you can use as a conversation opener," she said.

Those of us with dogs know how easy it is to meet people when we're walking the dogs, and many friends swear that it's one of the best ways to meet men (but you'd better really like dogs).

Listen Up

So who's right—is less effort better, when it comes to meeting men? Do good things happen when you're not expecting them or looking for them? Or is it better to have a game plan, or at least to put some effort into being in the right place at the right time? For those who believe some effort is necessary to get results, here are some ideas from the Marriage 100.

Ask your married friends for help. That's one of the best ways to meet men. "Married women always seem to know single men, either through their husbands or through their work. Ask them to keep an eye out for you," said one woman. Another said, "Most married women like to play matchmaker, especially if they're happily married themselves." "If you have a friend who's very social, a real outgoing person, ask her to help you, she'll love doing it," said another, who met her husband through such a person. "Two of my married girlfriends made it their business to find eligible men for me," said another. "Although there weren't a whole lot of men out there for me, those that I did meet were much more my type than those I met through singles groups."

Spread the word. In addition to your married friends, tell your friends and co-workers that you'd like to meet single men. But don't overdo it or you'll look desperate.

Get out, get busy, get involved. Most of the women stressed how important it is to "get out there" if you want to meet men. One said that she made up her mind that every day she would go somewhere or do something, outside of work, where she might meet men. It could be an art gallery, church, the gym, wherever, but it had to be something she honestly enjoyed where she might come in contact with men who enjoyed the same thing. Pursuing special interests is a great way to meet men, with the added advantage that if you don't meet that special someone, you've still enriched your life. "Be active and participate in as many group activities as possible," said a woman who met her husband taking a college language class.

Organize a singles party. I have a girlfriend who would give a party twice a year, for singles only. She would invite all her women friends and tell each of us to bring at least one male friend, someone we weren't dating. Her parties were lots of fun and she eventually married one of the men a friend brought to her party (and she was 50 when she met him). Another woman I know did something similar. She and three other friends each placed personal ads in a magazine, and then pooled their resources (and their little black books) and gave a party, inviting all the interesting men they met through the personals (and a few of their girlfriends, too, so the male-female ratio wouldn't be too lopsided). She married one of the men she met through that party.

Don't be shy. If you see someone who attracts you at a party, why wait for him to approach you? This is probably not an issue with younger women who have learned to be more assertive, but many older women were raised to play hard to get and to wait by the telephone or to be asked to dance. Don't. Also, even if you're shy, act as if you deserve the very best. Do this for every aspect of your life and notice how people respond favorably to such an attitude.

Look around you. "You may not have noticed him, but the right man for you may already be part of your life," said one. Others said, "Go on with an independent life and be open to someone who is nice"; "Be open to men who are different from the types that previously attracted you"; "Consider the types of men you may have rejected earlier. Look at them with fresh eyes"; "Get to know men who are different from the types that previously attracted you."

Be open to new experiences. "Focus on expanding your horizons and creating an interesting life for yourself, then watch how you'll attract interesting, new people into your life," said one woman. Another added, "Keep your mind active—take classes, read a lot, have lots of young friends, say yes to good things. You'll get a lot more out of life this way and you just might meet a man who's as interesting and as alive as you are."

Market yourself. Think of yourself as a product ready to fill a niche. Research the market, find the consumers, then pitch to them. Maybe that sounds cold and calculating but, hey, if it works for toothpaste, it can work for anything. So, figure out the type of man you'd like to spend the rest of your life with, think about where this type of man tends to hang out (health club, tennis courts, concerts, libraries, bowling alleys? All of the above?)

If these are places or activities that also interest you, then start your search there. Make yourself available. Remember, it takes careful planning to be in the right place at the right time.

Now that you're on your way to meeting the right man, it's time to think about how you'll handle your first date. Chances are, it'll be stressful—at least that was the experience of many of the Marriage 100—but not to worry, they survived and so will you. To find out how, read on.

CHAPTER 6

The First Date

Perhaps someday it will be pleasant to remember even this.

—VIRGIL

First dates are rarely easy, especially if you've been out of circulation for a while and have forgotten how to negotiate this often tortuous route. Unfortunately for all concerned, there is always a first date, in one form or another.

Jerry and I had our first date in an Irish restaurant, where he introduced me to Irish smoked salmon, which he claims is the best in the world (but then, he's Dublin-born, so what do you expect?). Personally, I hate fish of any kind, but I didn't want to offend him, so I ate it and agreed that, yes indeed, it was wonderful. That's the nature of first dates, isn't it? You're so anxious to please (at least I was) that you pretend to love something that you really hate. At the time he was a heavy smoker and I assured him that, no, it didn't bother me if he smoked. So, to be nice and make a good impression, I ate something I disliked, sitting in a smoking section, which I hate. But in all fairness, the conversation was great and we had a wonderful evening together, especially after my entree arrived—shepherd's pie, a real meat and potato dish that I love.

For most of the Marriage 100, the first date with their future husband was just as conventional—drinks, dinner, movies, or some combination of the three. Two women, however, threw caution to the wind, listened to their hearts and not their heads (or their friends, for that matter) and agreed to first dates that could have ended in disaster—and nearly did in one case. Both are first-time brides and you've met them earlier. One is Barbara, who struck up a correspondence with Charlie through Single Booklovers, and the other is Pat, the marketing executive, who met Pete on the job.

BARBARA

Take a chance and meet him on his turf

Barbara's first date with Charlie was a good lesson in trusting your instincts and not listening to your well-meaning but overanxious friends.

When Barbara started corresponding with Charlie, she lived in New York City and he lived some 300 miles north, near Buffalo. She was a public relations executive, he was a college math professor.

"When we started writing and I found out where he lived, I was a bit put off because the Buffalo area was the last place on earth where I wanted to end up," she said. Nevertheless, she wrote to Charlie regularly because she really enjoyed his letters. After three months of correspondence, he suggested they meet face-to-face.

"Your place or mine?" he wrote.

"Suddenly, a wave of anxiety washed over me," said Barbara. "I had been very comfortable just writing to him and trying to imagine what he looked like. We'd never exchanged photos or even talked on the telephone. A part of me wanted to keep it that way.

"Also, 'Your place or mine?' isn't so easy when it means one of us has to get on a train or drive a car for seven or eight hours," she continued. "I decided to throw caution to the wind and go up to his place. My friends went bersek, there were howls of protest. They thought I was crazy staying in a town so far from home, in the house of a man I only knew through letters. One friend, a judge who eventually married us, said, 'You should at least stay in a hotel or take a chaperon. What if he's crazy, a psychopath, an ax murderer?'

"They all thought it took real nerve, or stupidity, on my part to be going up there alone. But I didn't think so. I felt I knew him quite well. Besides, he assured me he had a spare bedroom where I could stay and I trusted him," she said. "I decided to go to his place and not have him come to my place because I think it's important to meet a man on his own turf. It helps you get a better picture of him and his lifestyle."

So, on a rainy Friday morning in late October, Barbara boarded a train to Buffalo, wearing a simple, slate grey wool dress that matched the color of the sky. She calls it her "comfort" dress because it's seen her through blind dates, job interviews and a host of other stressful situations. Her other fashion statement was a New York Yankees warmup jacket.

"I felt amazingly calm during the train ride," she said. "By that point, I was pretty philosophical about our meeting and I figured that, at the very least, I was going to have a pleasant weekend out of town."

When she stepped off the train and onto the station platform in Buffalo, she spotted Charlie right away.

"There weren't many people standing around there and fewer yet getting off the train, so we didn't have trouble finding each other. It was pleasant seeing him, but surprisingly unsurprising. I had formed a mental image of him that was very accurate, although I did envision twice as much hair," she said. "We were comfortable with each other from the very beginning.

"We drove to his house, about an hour away, and by the time we got there, I felt wonderfully relaxed. I knew I hadn't made a mistake," she said. "We already knew each other so well through our letters, and meeting him face to face simply confirmed all my good opinions of him."

On Saturday morning they drove to see the fall foliage and then to nearby Lake Erie, where they walked along the beach.

"It was cold and rainy and so-o-o-o romantic. Oh my God, it was fabulous," she said. "That Sunday, I returned to New York six feet off the ground. We had already made plans to spend Thanksgiving together and we started to talk about Christmas. It went very fast. It scared the bejesus out of me, but at the same time, it was remarkably comfortable."

She admits her one problem was that Charlie's town looked very much like her hometown, a tiny farming community in Ohio that she felt she'd outgrown years ago.

"My brother joined us at Thanksgiving and he kept walking around town saying, 'Oh my God, it looks like every small town in Ohio' and I'd say—my voice dripping with sarcasm—'Yes, I've observed that, thank you for sharing it.' Then, oblivious to my reaction, he'd spot another building and say something like, 'Oh my God, look at that bank building, it looks just like our old Citizens Bank.' Finally, I said, 'Enough already!'"

For Barbara and Charlie, dating meant taking turns commuting between New York and Buffalo on weekends.

"It wasn't easy," she said, "because it's an all-day trip, so if you leave on a Friday night and return on a Sunday, there's not much time to be together."

They were married in New York in 1992, by the same judge who originally feared Charlie might be an ax murderer. She was 42, he was 43. The only unhappy aspect of the marriage for Barbara was leaving New York, a city she loves deeply.

"It was wrenching. Even though I grew up in the Midwest, I'm a New Yorker to the core. I go into a frenzy if I can't find the Sunday *Times*, for example, and I've always grumbled about sloshing through snow and slush in the winter to get to the subway. Here, we're lucky if we can see above the snowbanks four months of the year. It just piles up and up and seems to stay forever, and I have to drive all over town to find a copy of the *Times*," she said.

"Living in this town is my only complaint. Fortunately, Charlie wants to move to New York eventually, so I'm patient. In the meantime, a day doesn't go by that I don't look at Charlie and marvel at the fact that he wasn't snatched up years ago."

PAT

When disaster strikes, talk it out

Pat, who had a lot to say about having anxiety attacks (Chapter 3), also has a lot to say about her first date with Pete. She admits she's a chance-taker and has a tendency to jump in over her head, so follow her lead only if you have nerves of steel and are prepared to accept rejection.

"Our first date was a nightmare," said Pat. "It almost derailed our entire relationship, personal and professional. That's partly because when he asked me for a date, I was thrown totally off guard.

"It happened when we were having one of our usual morning business calls, this one just before a three-day weekend. He asked me if I had plans for the weekend. I said I didn't know, thinking it was just a friendly inquiry."

Pat said the rest of the conversation went something like this:

Pete: "How would you like to go to the shore with me?"

Long pause.

Pat: "You mean, like a date?"

Pete: "Yeah."

Pat: "Like, you mean we're going to kiss goodnight?"

Pete: "Well, that was one of the things I had in mind."

"I was flabbergasted, speechless, and filled with conflicting emotions," said Pat. "I wondered, should I risk messing up a good friendship and a good working relationship, or should I take a chance on its turning into something even better?

"Finally, I said yes," she continued. "I figured we'd gotten along so beautifully that there must be something there. We'd been closely involved in business for months. I knew a lot about him and he knew a lot about me. Because there hadn't been any romantic pressure, we had formed a good, solid friendship.

"But the more I thought about it, the more nervous I became," she continued. "To make matters worse, I woke up with a urinary tract infection the Friday we were leaving and didn't have time to see a doctor. I just grabbed a quart of cranberry juice and gulped it down. The drive to the shore was a horror and set the stage for the entire weekend. We had to stop every half hour so I could go to the bathroom. By the time we checked into the hotel, I was totally wiped out."

Pat said she was so exhausted that she slept through Friday night and most of Saturday. By Saturday night, they were sitting across from each other in a seafood restaurant, with little appetite, both wishing they were somewhere else.

"He was polite, but I knew he was annoyed. Me? I was devastated. I kept saying to myself, 'What was I thinking, sharing a hotel room on a first date! Are you nuts, or what?' I was certain I had not only ruined a good friendship, but I was wondering whether we'd ever be able to work together again," she said.

But not to worry, the weekend had a happy ending, and the problems ended up being blessings in disguise.

"I woke up Sunday morning feeling a lot better. He, too, seemed in a better mood," she said. "Instead of heading straight home, which we had agreed to do the night before, we enjoyed a long, leisurely breakfast on the terrace, complete with champagne, and decided to stay another night.

"On our way home on Monday, I told Pete that if we can live through this, we can live through anything because we saw the worst side of each other and learned things that it usually takes months of living together to learn about someone," she said. "And we learned it all in just three days.

"When I look back on that weekend, I don't know how we got through it," she said. "It was a very good learning experience, to say the least. We learned, among other things, that we're diametrically opposite in our sleep patterns. I'm a morning person, in bed by 10:00 and up at 6:00. He's a night hound, who's up till midnight and can't open his eyes before 10:00. He saw what kind of mood I get in when I'm sick, or when I'm tired. I learned what happens when he doesn't get his way—we learned those things in one short weekend. It was all compressed and totally disconcerting.

"I would not recommend this kind of first date," she continued. "In fact, I would not wish those first two days on anyone. My advice is, take it a bit slower than we did. There are just too many things that can go wrong." On the other hand, all's well that ends well.

FRAN
Appearances can be deceiving

Remember Fran, who met her toupee-wearing husband at Disney World? If you'll recall, he was doing research for a book about whether being bald handicaps men in the dating game. He promised to call, but she didn't really care whether she heard from him again once she returned to New York.

"We left Orlando on different flights. Although I gave him my phone number, my attitude was, 'If he calls when we get back, that's fine, if not, that's fine, too.'"

He called two days later saying, almost breathlessly, "I've *got* to see you."

"I thought that was a bit strange, since we didn't know each other that well," said Fran. "'I've *got* to see you,'??? There was a sense of urgency in that statement that I thought was really weird. But I said OK. We went out to dinner and over dinner he told me he was wearing a toupee and that when we got back to my apartment he was going to take it off," she said. Fran admits she found this conversation also a little weird and was beginning to wonder about this guy.

"This toupee obsession was starting to get to me," she said, adding that he got even weirder when they returned to her apartment.

"He disappeared into the bathroom for about ten minutes. My cat, Biscuit, was sitting on a table near the bathroom door, watching him," she continued. "When Craig came out of the bathroom, he took one look at the cat and, instead of coming straight into the living room where I was sitting, he bolted into the hallway where his coat was hanging on a hook and put his hairpiece in his coat pocket. I think he was afraid Biscuit would pounce on it."

Fran said that when Craig came into the living room, with bald head gleaming, he seemed much more relaxed, as if a weight had been lifted off of him, quite literally.

"I said, 'Now that's much better, isn't it?' I told him, in my most reassuring tone, that he looked just fine bald, and I meant it. He was really relieved by my reaction. The ironic part is, my first husband wore a hairpiece and was obsessive about it. He wouldn't let me see him without it, not even in bed. Craig loves the fact that my first husband wore a hairpiece. Does all of this seem odd? I don't know, it wasn't any odder than most of the dates I've had in New York."

Stella

Don't worry about age

Stella, a teacher who believes, "You meet men by doing things you enjoy," proves her point by relating how she first got involved with her second husband, Carl.

She was spending two weeks at a summer camp for adults and families in the mountains of New Hampshire when she met and fell in love with Carl. It was her fourth visit in as many years.

"Carl was in the process of a divorce and was there with his three young children that summer. He went there every year and recalled meeting me there about four years before. I only had a vague recollection of meeting him, probably because in previous years he was there with his wife.

She said their relationship began one afternoon when she was watching Carl and others play volleyball. She was sitting on the sidelines, oblivious of the fact that he was watching her while she was watching them.

"He told me later he noticed me on the sidelines and said that the minute he looked at me, he knew we were going to get involved. After the game, he came over and introduced himself and invited me to join him on a hike with his kids. I went hiking with them every day after that, and we all had a wonderful time.

Stella is ten years older than Carl and, at the time, she was afraid it might be a problem.

"That summer I was 45 and he was 35 and I felt self-conscious about being several years older, even though I look much younger than my age," she said. "I told him my age the first evening we were together. He said it didn't make any difference to him what my age was, so I relaxed about it.

"The second night we took a walk alone together along a hill-top above the camp. It was so romantic—a clear, star-filled night. We walked and talked for a long time, and then we headed back down the hill toward the lights of the camp, with thousands of stars twinkling overhead," she said. "Carl pointed to the sky and said our meeting each other was 'written in the stars.' It was so romantic, such a lovely thing to say. I've never forgotten it.

"Of course, he wanted to go to bed with me that night, but I said no because's there's no real privacy at the camp," she continued.

"The walls are too thin. The rooms are in old farmhouses and old lodges and you hear everything. I'm very modest and shy that way."

A few days later Carl asked Stella to go off alone with him to Monhegan Island, off the coast of Maine. He wanted to leave the camp because his (soon-to-be) ex-wife was arriving to join the kids and Carl wanted to leave right after she arrived and gathered them.

"I left with him and you could say our first real date was a week on Monhegan Island. It's a charming place, an artist's colony full of galleries. It was very romantic and it's where we made love for the first time. When we returned to Boston, he moved in with me and we've been together ever since." They were married two years later.

KAREN

Go out no matter what your mood

Karen, the widow who rewed at 67, believes in forcing yourself to get out and circulate, no matter how depressed or anxious you may feel. She's the one who met her second husband at her first husband's funeral.

"After my husband's funeral I went away for two months with some of my children and grandchildren to a small house we had in Santa Fe," she said. "When I returned home, there was a message from Jack on my answering machine, saying he'd like to have lunch with me to discuss a publishing project he was involved in, since he knew I was a published writer.

"I called back and we set a date and place," she continued. "He picked a rather dinky restaurant in a crummy part of town. Very unromantic. It was a neighborhood, I'm happy to say, I was delightedly unfamiliar with. Our appointment was for 12:30. When I drove into the parking lot, the attendant told me I had to be back by three, their closing time. I said, 'No problem, I'll be back by 1:30 or 2:00 at the latest.'

"I remember walking up the street pushing one foot in front of the other, wondering, 'What am I doing here? I don't give a damn about his project,'" she said. "Then I thought, 'Well, where else would you rather be?' And the fact was, there was no other place where I wanted to be, because way down deep I knew I wanted to get to know Jack better."

Karen admits she saw it more as a date than a business meeting, even though she was too newly widowed to think about another man romantically.

They met in a small Chinese restaurant where they both ordered the shrimp with ginger and then began to talk nonstop.

"He talked about his wife who had died a few months before and I talked about my husband and we both began to cry, and as we talked, we suddenly heard this sort of weird sound like a vacuum cleaner. I turned around and, my God, it *was* a vacuum cleaner. The restaurant was totally empty and it was well past three," she said. "We left and ran to the parking lot—luckily it was still open. I was the last one out."

She said Jack left the next day for a ten-day business trip, but he called her every night while he was away.

"When he returned, he came over to take me to the movies, but we never got to the movies," she said, with a wink. They were married six months later. She was 67, he was 72.

REBECCA

Be prepared for pleasant surprises

Rebecca, a single mom who wed a co-worker, learned on her first date with him that a man's after-work personality can be totally different from his office persona.

"Dan and I worked together in a marketing firm. He was a widower with grown children," she said. "People would tease me, saying he was single and available, but I'd say, 'You've got to be kidding, the man has no sense of humor. I know he has four kids, but I don't think he knows how he got them."

Although they worked closely together, nearly three years passed before he asked her out for a drink after work.

"I didn't really want to go, but I said, 'OK, just one drink and then I have to get home to feed my two kids,'" she continued.

"We went to a lounge nearby and started talking about a project we were working on together. Before you knew it, we ordered something to eat and we sat and talked about ourselves and our children for three hours. I was totally surprised by his after-work personality. I realized he's very easy to talk to and does, indeed, have a sense of humor—albeit a very dry one.

"That was the night I thought he had possibilities as a lover, but I was reluctant to get involved with anyone at work," she said. "Nevertheless, we started having drinks and dinner together on a regular basis after work. There was no pressure, we simply enjoyed each other's company, but as the relationship started to turn serious, I began to get nervous.

"Having been there once before, I wasn't too anxious to make the same mistake a second time and I told him so," she continued. "I reminded him that he had been happily married for twenty years, but I'd had twelve years of a miserable marriage, so I wanted to go slow."

After that, we saw each other constantly and spent weekends together and got to know each other's families. Finally, I felt sure this one would be a happy one." They were married six months later. She was 50, he was 52.

LENORE
Keep the train schedules handy

Lenore, as you may recall, met Jake through a personal ad she placed after having met so many men that weren't right for her that she was about to give up.

"We talked on the phone for about three hours before we agreed to meet," she said. "He came out on the Long Island Railroad, about a two-hour ride, and I agreed to meet the train. As I sat in my car watching people get off the train, I said to myself, 'If this guy gets off carrying a shopping bag, I'm driving away.' Don't ask me why, but so many of the men who answered my ad got off the train carrying shopping bags."

Luckily for both of them, he was not carrying a shopping bag. When Lenore spotted him, the first thought that ran through her mind was, 'Oh boy, he looks young, sexy, and attractive.'

"So many of the others just looked tired and worn out. Jake didn't—he looked full of energy. Also, he had a lot of hair and I liked that," she said.

They went to a restaurant near the train station for dinner so he could take an evening train back into New York. Unfortunately, neither was familiar with the train schedules.

"We had a wonderful dinner together and when it came time for him to go, he pulled out his train schedule and realized that he had just missed a train and another one wasn't due for over an hour," she said. "I told him he could stay over at my house, and sleep in the den. I felt very comfortable inviting him home. There was no awkwardness between us; it was as if we were old friends. At the time I had three daughters at home, the oldest was 14, and they were all asleep when we arrived.

"Jake and I made up the bed in the den—he wanted sex, but I said no and went upstairs to my own bedroom," she said.

Lenore said the next morning, when her 11-year-old daughter passed by the den on the way to the bathroom, she noticed that the door was partially open and saw Jake in bed. Without skipping a beat, she said, "Good morning, would you like a cup of coffee or tea?"

"Jake was shocked at how nonchalant she was about the whole thing," said Lenore. "Later he asked me, 'Does this happen a lot in your house? Your daughter wasn't even surprised to see a strange man sleeping in the den.' I told him that it had never happened before, and that was the truth, but my kids were pretty sophisticated even then, and very little shocked them." Lenore and Jake were married three years later. She was 41, he was 36.

DOLORES
Be cool and aloof

Dolores, you'll recall, is the 64-year-old widow who met her husband, John, in a Bible study group. She's a big believer in asking friends to keep an eye out for you.

"I'm old-fashioned about meeting men—I believe in being introduced by someone you know," she said. "Luckily for me, I had a very social friend who loved to play matchmaker.

"My friend and her husband, and John and I were members of a Bible study group that met once a week," she said. "I found John very interesting, but I was too shy to do anything about it. One day I told my friend that I was attracted to John and she went into action. She was convinced that John and I were right for each other.

"She arranged for us to have a double date with her and her husband," she continued. "The four of us went out to dinner together and then to her house to play cards. I had a lovely time. I liked John a lot and was quite excited about our date, but I tried not to show it. I was very cool and polite, even though inside I felt as giddy as a teenager."

In fact, she admits she was all aflutter, especially when John held her hand in the back seat of the car, as they were on their way to dinner.

"When John took my hand I thought, 'Goodness, we're just on a first date,'" she said. "I was very shy about those things, but I was also thrilled."

The evening was obviously a big success because after that, John called her every day and they met for lunch or dinner several times a week. They were married six months later, both for the second time.

Here are a few other examples of first dates that some of the Marriage 100 enjoyed (or didn't enjoy) with their future husbands:

Alice: Straight to bed: "I invited him over for a drink a week after we met. We were in bed within a half-hour." Alice, if you'll recall, wed for the fifth time at 51.

Carrie: Took him to dinner: "Tony had been my physician for fifteen years, or so. We got to know each other outside that relationship when he helped me with a car problem one Saturday morning on the main street of town. He just happened to be driving by when my car broke down. A month later, I took him out to dinner as thanks for his helpfulness." They were married seven months later, both for the second time. She was 46.

Noreen: Took own car, just in case: "I first met Fred at a party at a friend's home in San Francisco, when both of us were vacationing there. He had a wife at the time, but a year later, when we both happened to be in San Francisco again, he showed up alone, told me he was divorced, and asked me out to dinner. I suggested we meet at a restaurant. I wanted my wheels so I wouldn't get stuck after dinner if he was boring." He wasn't boring. They were wed eight months later, both for the second time. Noreen was 48.

Joanna: A 24-hour date: "I met Ernest at a Mensa social. I joined to meet intelligent women and found an intelligent man instead. We got together the following day. Our date lasted twenty-four hours—you may infer what you will." They were wed two years later. Joanna was 47 and it was her first marriage.

Helna: We talked all night: "We grew up in the same town in Holland and had dated each other for four years when we were in our 20s. We drifted apart. He stayed in Europe, I moved to the USA, and we both married someone else and raised a family. When I went home for a visit, George was still there. We hadn't seen each other for twenty-two years, and by then we were both divorced. He invited me to a folk festival and then dinner, and we just talked and talked all night. It was sheer joy. We hugged and laughed and had a wonderful time, as if we'd never been separated." They were married two years later and moved to the Southwest together. Helna was 46.

Paula: Felt like a teenager: "I was a little nervous when Mike picked me up. We had dinner at a very fine restaurant. I thought he was really great and probably very wealthy—I felt like a teenager, like I was walking on air. Many years later I found out he had borrowed the dinner money from a friend." They were wed eight months later, both for the second time. She was 41.

Does any of this sound familiar? The way you feel on your first date with a guy when you're 16 probably isn't all that different from how you feel when you're 45 and the mother of three. If you were nervous as a teenager (and who wasn't?), you're probably going to be nervous now. The important thing to remember is that whatever disaster might occur, it'll probably be something to laugh about years later.

Listen Up

Judging from some of the advice parceled out, some things never change. So much of what the Marriage 100 have to say is as valid today as it was when our mothers were dating. If you heed some of these timeless tips, you'll undoubtedly have more fun, and maybe you'll even end up with the type of guy who's right for you.

Be yourself. This advice came up again and again. It just doesn't pay to play games—to play hard to get, feign interest, or pretend to be something you're not only attracts a man who's looking for those qualities and expects you to be that way on the second, third, and fourth dates—if the relationship gets that far. Here's what four of the women had to say: "Too many women seem willing to give up their individuality to hook up with someone; that's a big mistake in the long run"; "Don't play helpless or be self-effacing"; "Be the best you can be and be proud of it"; "Know you deserve the best, don't act like he's doing you a favor by taking you out."

Take a chance. So many women, especially divorced women or those who've had long, painful relationships, are afraid to take a chance on a man because it hurts so much to be rejected. They simply don't want to risk going through all that pain again. But if you don't take that first step and go on that first date, you'll never know if this might be the right man for you. Besides, even if he's not right for you, maybe he has a friend.

Listen carefully. There's an old saying that God gave man two ears and one tongue so he'd listen twice as much as he talks. Good advice for women, too, especially on a first date. You can learn a lot more about someone by listening than by talking.

Look as good as you can. While we all want to be appreciated for our inner beauty, packaging *is* important, let's not kid ourselves. If necessary, lose weight, get a makeover or a new hairstyle, update your wardrobe. Not just because you want to please a man, but because you'll feel better about yourself—and the better you feel about yourself, the more appealing you'll be to others.

Keep it light. Above all, have fun. It's only a date, it's not the rest of your life. Or is it?

Now that you're ready to weather the first of many dates, let's fast-forward to some of those big decisions you'll need to make *before* the wedding day (or wish you had, if you don't). How do you know this is really the right guy for you? What type of wedding do you want? How will you handle finances—his and her accounts, or share everything? It can get complicated. Let's move on and take a look at what some of the Marriage 100 have to say about their own wedding day, lessons they learned from their ex-husbands (among others), and how they handle the money issues.

CHAPTER 7

Before You Say "I Do"

Hope for miracles but don't rely on one.

—YIDDISH PROVERB

He may be a great friend and lover, but how do you know he'll make a good husband? In the first section, *Stop! Look! Listen!* we'll hear from women who think it's a big mistake to simply follow your heart and "go for it." They'll tell us when *not* to "go for it" and why. They'll also tell us what they've learned from past mistakes, and what they think are important qualities to look for in a man.

What are some of the clues that tell you about a man's character? How can you be certain he's the right one for you? And if he's not, when do you cut your losses and run?

Here's what a few have to say:

"Look closely at how he treats his ex-wife because it's an indication of how he'll treat you," said one woman. For another, the important word is *know*, as in "Know your needs, and know your partner and his family very, very well before you take that leap."

In the second section, *Love and Money*, we'll hear how some of these women and their husbands ironed out the money matters *before* the wedding. We're not talking prenuptial agreements here (that comes later, in Chapter 8), we're talking about everyday spending and savings patterns. Some believe you should keep your money separate from his, have your own checking accounts, keep your property in your own name. Others say the opposite. We'll look at the reasons behind their opinions. We'll also hear from one who blames money problems for the breakup of her marriage. She hopes she can help others avoid the mistakes she made.

The last section, *Say "I Do" Your Way,* looks at the different types of weddings enjoyed by these women. Some had traditional, full-blown weddings, with their kids and grandkids in attendance, others (myself included) ran off to City Hall to avoid the stress of a wedding, and one was wed at a nudist colony, because, among other things, "I didn't have to worry about what to wear."

Stop! Look! Listen!

Do we learn from past failures or are we always destined to repeat them? Many of the women in this survey did, indeed, learn some important lessons from previous, failed marriages, and they were determined not to travel that path again.

When I asked the women who'd been widowed or divorced to describe how their current marriage differs from previous marriages, practically all of them said that this one is very different because their needs are radically different. Most had already raised a family or were beyond the age of wanting to have children. The majority said that in this marriage, companionship was more important than sex, that as they got older and, hopefully, wiser, a man's looks, career, and income, were not nearly as important as his kindness, generosity, and temperament.

One advantage of an older marriage is that there are usually no questions about having more children, or what religion to practice, or whose career gets priority. These are issues you've usually worked out by the time you reach 40, with or without a husband. As one 48-year-old bride said, "In this marriage I can allow for more 'space' and for greater differences. Thinking alike is just not as important when you're older, primarily because you're not planning to raise a family together."

Learning from the Ex-husband(s)

Needless to say, with the divorced women, none of the former husbands compared favorably to the current one. But most women took away lessons from previous marriages that helped them make better choices the second (or third or fourth) time around. Perhaps Julie, who wed for the second time at 42, sums it up best:

- Remember everything you disliked in your first marriage and make sure you don't repeat the same mistakes.
- Find a new type—if a certain type was wrong for you the first time around, he'll be wrong for you the second or third time around.
- Make sure your intended will help fulfill your desires and vice versa.

Lenore
Find one who likes to talk

Finding a good communicator was a big one for Lenore, who was previously married to a man who never expressed his feelings. The "silent type" is definitely not her type.

"Look for a man's ability to communicate. He needs to be able to talk to you about what's bothering him," said Lenore, the Long Island divorcee who met Jake, her second husband, through the personals. "My first husband never liked to talk. He was not in touch with his feelings. We were never able to communicate. Jake is different, he's very open. He's a talker and not afraid to express his feelings—sometimes he talks too much, but I prefer that to his not talking enough. I looked for that in a man, because I know how difficult life can be with someone who doesn't want to talk about what's bugging him and expects you to be a mind reader."

GINNY
Find one who's fun

Ginny, who wed for the second time at 45, said, "My husband and I have a very nurturing relationship. We are partners in everything. My first marriage was extremely destructive and competitive. We never laughed together, it wasn't fun. We were always finding fault with each other and putting each other down. The fact is, we didn't like each other very much, but we never acknowledged it, not even to ourselves.

"The first time around I was 34 and I thought I knew all the things that were important to look for in a man, but I really didn't have a clue," she continued. "One important lesson I learned is that you can't expect the man you marry to make you feel good about yourself. That is something you have to do on your own. And don't expect him to fish you out of an unhappy or boring life. Don't expect to change him, either. But do find a man you can have fun with, someone who can share your sense of humor, because being able to laugh together is very important."

Ginny met Duane in the elevator of the building where they both live in New York. Two months later they went out to dinner in the neighborhood.

"He seemed nice, but I wasn't sure he was my type. He's fourteen years older. I had always been attracted to adolescent personalities, probably because I was afraid to grow up myself," she said. "Duane seemed mature and, at first, I wasn't sure I knew how to handle that. After I got to know him, I realized how great it is to be with an adult, and one who's fun, to boot."

Fay

Think before you leap

"A lot of serious thought should go into a second marriage. We don't give much thought to the first marriage because when we're young, we usually let our heart rule our head," said Fay, who wed for the first time at 20 and for the second time at 45. "If you're contemplating marriage, think twice, do not rush and, above all else, don't marry just because you're lonely. Learn to analyze your needs before you get seriously involved with a man again."

She said that in her first marriage, neither she nor her husband knew how to communicate their feelings, something she thinks can sink a marriage. He also insisted on making all the major decisions and rarely discussed them with her.

"When I was hurt, I would get angry and this would get in the way of our talking it out. Also, I needed his confirmation of my worth, instead of building up my own sense of worth," she said. "My first marriage lasted twenty-two years and we had two children, but it was never a happy marriage.

"My second husband is very close to his feelings and expresses them easily," said Fay. "He wants to please me and make me happy, and part of that is he won't make any major decisions without discussing them with me."

Linda

Avoid the jealous type

One of the lessons Linda learned from her first marriage is that life with a possessive man is a life of hell, full of restrictions, suspicions, and always having to explain yourself. She was determined not to make the same mistake the second time around.

"My first husband was an insecure, controlling, jealous, mean, and abusive man. As a result, I pulled away from him emotionally. I was terrified of provoking his anger," said Linda, the mother of four who wed for the second time at 48. "My first marriage was so restrictive. With my ex-husband, if I so much as looked at another man, it blew his mind. After the children were in school, I decided to go back to college and take a few classes. Even that bothered him, he was so afraid I might meet other men. Another thing that upset him was my going skiing once a week with a group of women from our country club. He knew the women, but he just couldn't believe that any of this was innocent.

"He didn't like my doing anything for myself. If my activities didn't involve him, the children, or the house, he got very angry," she said. "He was totally selfish."

Linda said her second husband, Don, is just the opposite and has encouraged her to be independent and have a life and career of her own.

"He likes women who have lives of their own, women who don't cling. He encourages me to do things that interest me, to enjoy my own circle of friends," she said. "Marriage to Don is a partnership in all ways. We give each other a lot of freedom to pursue our own individual endeavors. He is never abusive—he's always in a good mood, confident, and supportive."

EMILY

You must both learn to clear the air

Emily, who met David on a blind date and wed for the third time at 45, said the most important thing she learned from her past marriages is this: You must clear the air before you wed, because whatever problems exist will get worse, not better, after marriage.

"I used to withdraw into myself when there was a problem. I picked men who were the same way," she said. "I never had open discussions with either of my two ex-husbands. Now I know to stand up and fight, to clear the air.

"Don't run from problems. Stand firm and deal with them," she continued. If you don't, you'll be heading for trouble. It's hard to let go of bad habits, especially if they seemed to work for you in the past. But the gain in sticking with old patterns is usually only short-term. If you're the type who withdraws into yourself when there's a problem, work on learning to express your feelings before you even think of getting married. Do it on your own or get professional help, but do it. It can make all the difference between a happy and an unhappy marriage. Luckily, in this marriage, we've both learned the importance of expressing our feelings honestly, something neither of us did in previous relationships."

Emily also believes you have to be true to yourself and not give up hard-won financial and emotional independence.

"Choose to make this new relationship work for both of you without giving up what you've spent years building, such as personal growth or a sense of worth," she said. "For me, the biggest change came from the conviction that I can stand up for myself. I never did that before."

GLENDA
Be careful what you ask for

Glenda, who wed for the second time at 48, is a good example of that old saying, "Be careful what you ask for, you might get it."

"My first husband was a sportaholic and was always away at some sporting event or other," she said. "My present husband likes sports, too, but it's not an obsession with him. Trouble is, he won't go anywhere without me, to a sports event or anywhere else. This, too, is a problem, because I've gone from one extreme to the other—from always being alone to never being alone. I love him very much, but I do wish he'd take up a hobby of some kind. There has to be a happy medium."

What You See Is What You Get

Practically all of the women had a variation on the theme that you can't expect to change a man after you're married to him (or at any time in a relationship, for that matter). Here's a sprinkling of their opinions and observations:

- "Remember that old saying, 'The things that bother you before you marry, only get worse afterward.'"
- "Accept him as is, that's vital to a happy marriage."
- "If you don't like what you see, and you don't think you can live with it, find someone else."
- "You can't change them, don't even try."

ANNETTE

Know that love does not conquer all

"Marriage works for you in mid-life when you know each other well enough that you understand what you're getting into and what the compromises are going to be," said Annette, the writer who wed for the first time at 44. "When you're younger, you don't think about these kinds of things. Then when problems crop up, you have these horrible situations, usually due to the fact that you closed your eyes to your differences and thought that 'Love conquers all.' It doesn't.

"Before we were married, Marv said to me, 'My God, you ask questions I had never even thought about.' I replied, 'I only intend to do this once and I intend to be happy while I'm doing it.'" (Annette also has plenty to say on finances, later in this chapter.)

GLORIA

Expect lots of adjustments

"Marriage is a frightening prospect but worth it." Gloria, a mother of two, wed for the third time at 40. Her husband, David, was 50, also divorced with two children. They met through work.

"Although we had both been emotionally and financially battered in the breakup of our two previous marriages, we never abandoned the ideals of what makes for a true marriage," she said.

"What we have in this marriage, which I think is unique to older marriages, is that we are friends and companions first. Another plus in this marriage is the lack of competition between us, which I also think is more typical of older marriages than of younger ones."

JOYCE
Get flexibility

"With all your getting, get flexibility."

That's the advice of Joyce, the divorcee you met earlier who wed for the second time at 50.

"As we age, we should become more flexible and be more easy-going, not more set in our ways," she said. "You must be willing to look at your future husband's point of view and be willing to accommodate differences of opinion. And he should do the same for you. Also, I don't believe that opposites attract, at least I don't believe that relationships between opposites are happy ones. It's important to have a lot in common because sharing is a very important element in a good marriage. People don't suddenly become wild about something you like, just because you like it. And don't fake it by pretending to be wild about something he likes, because in the long run it won't work."

GINNY
Learn to cool it

"You must have patience and understanding if you plan to marry later in life. He has his ways, you have yours," said Ginny, who wed for the third time at 49. "Keep your mouth shut when you see those little, irritating habits of his. Undoubtedly, you have some that will bother him. Don't make a big thing of it; it's not all that important."

KATHLEEN
Take your time

"Before you decide to marry a particular man, be certain you're truly compatible," said Kathleen, who wed for the second time at 41. "Remember, this is the man you'll probably share your retirement years with. Can you get along when neither of you is rushing off to work in the morning or busy with children?

"Companionship means more when you're older, even if you're not yet retired. You're not totally caught up in raising a family or following a career path, or both, as you usually are in your 20s and 30s," she said. "You have more time to be with each other, but this can be a mixed blessing. Being compatible doesn't just mean being together, it also means giving each other space. Before you marry, let him know about the activities you probably won't share with him, things you like to do alone or with friends, that you'll want to continue pursuing. Encourage him to do the same. Why should either of you give up old friends or things you enjoy, just because you're getting married and your partner has no interest?

"Also, wait until the sexual intimacies are comfortable and have a pattern to them, to see if you're happy with that side of the relationship," she said. "All this takes time."

Oh, and one more piece of advice from Kathleen: "Have him agree to have a vasectomy."

Love and Money

Tackling the money issues can be a daunting task. Here's how some of the women did it.

GLADYS AND RAUL
Do the finances together

With older couples, it's often the husband who takes care of the finances and the wife who goes along with it. In the case of Gladys and Raul, the opposite is true. Gladys controls the finances, and she isn't the least bit happy about it.

"Be sure that you share the financial concerns, that you don't get stuck paying all the bills and being totally responsible for balancing the checkbook," said Gladys, who wed for the second time at 44. "I learned this the hard way, because if Raul and I have one problem, it's my resentment of being the family bookkeeper. Raul is from the old school, he goes out and works and hands the paycheck over to me ('Just pay the bills,' he says). If things have to be juggled, he doesn't want to know about it. As long as everything is going smoothly, there's no problem, but if we have to dig into our savings, he gets mad and wants to know what I did wrong.

"When we married, we pooled our resources and combined everything, including a nice settlement from my divorce. That part has worked out fine. What isn't working out fine is my being responsible for the day-to-day finances," she said. "I wish we had worked this out before we got married."

PEGGY AND IAN
She handles the finances

In Peggy's case, her handling all the finances suits her husband just fine. Peggy loves it and is good at it, Ian hates it and always made a mess of it.

"I take care of the finances, by mutual consent," she said. "He said if he were to do it, he would probably have to take time off from work every month. It took me five months to balance his checkbook. What a mess. I closed that account and now we pool our resources and put our money in joint accounts. The arrangement works just fine for us."

JO AND ANDREW
Have his and her accounts

About half the women believe in joint accounts, the other half believe in separate accounts. Jo is of the latter school and she's probably fairly typical of women who are used to handling their own money and like it that way.

"We have a common account for household expenses and in addition, I have my own account and he has his," said Jo, the teacher and Francophile who wed for the second time at 48. "Before Andrew and I married, we never discussed how we'd handle money, it just worked out this way. I never see his checking account and vice versa. Andrew doesn't have the slightest idea what I spend and he doesn't care.

"Handling my own money is very important to me," she continued. "I was single and on my own for more than twenty years before I met Andrew and remarried, so I was used to handling my own money. I've worked since I was 13 and have never asked anyone for permission on how to spend my money. It isn't something I would want to start doing at this stage in my life."

JULIE AND SCOTT
Combine everything

"We combine everything and it works out fine," said Julie, who wed for the second time at 42. "I think having his and her accounts could make life very complicated. If you earn less than he does or you're a stay-at-home-wife, how do you divide up the money fairly?"

Linda and Don
Give according to income

Linda has the answer to Julie's question of how to split up the income in a fair and equitable way when one partner earns much more than the other.

"We have a financial arrangement where we each contribute to the household according to our income," she said. "He makes a lot more than I do, so it's about a 65-35 split. In our wills, his share goes to his kids, my share goes to my kids. Except for our wills, we don't have anything in writing, but we haven't had any problems."

Annette and Marv
Remember the alimony

Women who complain about their husband's alimony bills could learn a lesson from Annette.

"I married a man who has a $3000 per month alimony bill, which is horrific. When it upsets me, I say to myself, 'This is something he wanted to do, because his ex-wife had taken very good care of the children. I see it as a positive thing because I think that how a man treats his ex-wife is a good indication of how he will treat his next wife.

"Marv didn't feel that his ex should suffer because he was no longer there to provide financially," she continued. "She got the house, and the high alimony for six years, then the alimony figure starts dropping. He gave more than the court would have demanded and I respect him for that."

Annette is typical of women who are uncomfortable with the idea of relying on another person for money. She was very independent and felt she had her finances under control when Marv entered her life and upset her carefully laid out plans.

"When I left my job to write a book, I had enough money to last two years, just enough to pay the mortgage on my condo, my car note, feed myself, and have a little extra. I had been saving up for this and had it all very carefully calculated," she said. "For the first year I lived off my savings. I was into the second year of my savings when Marv and I fell in love and he came to live with me. By then I had just enough money left for the next seven months. When he moved in, he paid rent and paid for entertainment when we went out. He wanted to pay more, but I said no. I'm very independent. I figure if I don't owe you, I can say and do what I want. I was very strict about maintaining control of my condo and my money.

Those carefully laid plans went down the tubes when Annette and Marv decided to get married.

"I splurged and spent the last of my savings on our wedding. It meant that I had no money left, and that made me nervous. Marv told me, 'You can either go back to office work or you can continue writing and let me support you.'

"Well, what would you do if you were given that choice? I said yes, but it was a dilemma for me because writing full-time meant that I had no money to maintain a separate checking account and that was important to me symbolically," she said. "For a while I kept one anyway, but it was costing me money because if you don't keep a certain minimum in an account, they charge you—so, in effect, I was paying the bank to keep my account open. I thought that was crazy and closed the account after a few months."

Annette said she then had to depend on Marv for all her expenses. He gave willingly, but it drove her crazy.

"I have great difficulty asking for money," she said. "He would give me a certain amount each month, and more if I asked, but I wouldn't ask for more. After a few months of that, I decided to get a part-time teaching job—it only pays $15,000 a year, which I dump into the general household account, but I feel so much better contributing something.

"With most of us, when it comes to money there are so many different things going on all at once, on so many different levels.

How you handle money in a marriage is a very complex, individual thing. Luckily, we don't have a power problem—you know how they talk about money being a symbol of power. It is with a lot of people and that can lead to big problems in a marriage, especially if one partner earns much more than the other.

"Be sure you've worked out these issues in advance, and never think that because you earn less, you're not entitled to the same input as your husband about how money is spent," she said.

MARLENE AND JASON
Protect your piece of the pie

"Always have separate accounts. Always. Don't give the whole pie away. I have a friend who is constantly lending money to her live-in lover—she makes a lot more than he does, and he's always spending her money and promising to pay it back, but he never does," said Marlene, who wed for the second time at 42. "Once the money is spent, it's hard to get it back, no matter how close your relationship. My friend and her lover have terrible fights over money, and it always gets in the way of their enjoying each other. Don't let it happen to you."

Marlene suggests having three accounts marked, "Ours," "Hers," and "His." Like Linda, she suggests you deposit money into each account according to your income.

"You must have an account of your own to feel comfortable spending money and not having to ask permission every time you buy something," she said. "It's especially hard for women who don't earn much or who are full-time homemakers to feel they can spend money freely. Even when everything is pooled and your husband is generous, you tend to think of the money as 'his' money. Have access to your own money, and spend it as you please.

"These are issues that must be decided in advance," she continued. "There's no right or wrong way of doing things. How you handle finances is very personal and you both must be comfortable with the arrangement or there'll be trouble ahead. When you're not in it together, you can end up with real problems."

Marlene knows what she's talking about. Her first husband was a tyrant about money and made her feel guilty about spending "His" money.

"Every month when the bank statement arrived, he would sit with me, as if I were a child, and ask me about every check I wrote," she said. "I was always exhausted at the end of it. He did this every single month. I think he did it deliberately to intimidate me, and it worked because I found it very demeaning."

SUSAN AND LENNY
Problems loom if you don't share

Susan and Lenny share everything, but they don't think they're typical.

"Everything we own is in both our names, but I know a lot of couples where that's not the case," said Susan, who wed for the first time at 40. "A friend of ours has a marriage where he moved into her house and it's still 'her' house and not 'their' house. My husband and I are open and free about sharing everything. When we wed, I moved into his house and he said right off that it was our house, not just his any longer. I couldn't have dealt with it if he had said it was his house. When that happens, you never feel you belong."

FRAN AND CRAIG
Marry a generous man

"Until this marriage I'd spent my entire life worrying about money," said Fran, the writer and artist, who wed for the second time at 45. "Craig gets very aggravated with me if I mention I need money for something. He just says, 'Get it.'

"I have my own checking account, mainly because Craig doesn't want to worry about how I spend money," said Fran. "He makes a lot more than I do, but he always reminds me that everything is ours. I can't complain—I put money into my account and take money out of our joint account. Not a bad deal."

PHYLLIS AND MIKE, HEATHER AND AL
Money led to breakup

Money was the villain in two cases where the marriages did not work out. Phyllis's marriage to Mike, the second marriage for both of them, ended in divorce after fifteen years. Heather and Al, have separated after a twelve-year marriage. It was her second, his third. In both cases, they blame money problems.

"Money. Oh Lord! Money was a big problem," said Phyllis, who was 41 when she wed Mike. "Mike was heavily in debt when we married, but I didn't know it. Because he was a big spender, I assumed he could afford the luxury apartment he lived in as a bachelor, the nice restaurants he took me to when we started dating. He told me he owed the IRS $15,000—I thought that anyone who owed the IRS that kind of money must have a large income. He was extremely creative, a lot of fun, but after we married, I ended up supporting him. We lived high. He was a self-employed graphic artist and sometimes he'd get a big job and be on the verge of becoming a millionaire, but he couldn't follow through. I stupidly gave him all of my money and put everything I had in both our names—a big mistake. He put money in our joint account when he earned it, but I was the one who really supported us on a steady basis. We stayed together for twelve years, but I finally got fed up with his going through all my savings. It was money problems that broke up this marriage, no doubt about it.

"Yet, the truth is, if you're in love, you don't think about those things," she said. "You enter a marriage with a feeling of trust—and that's the way it should be, but I guess I was a bit too trusting."

Phyllis offers two important pieces of advice so you don't end up the same way, "Before you marry, check him out financially, and secure some money of your own, in an account he can never touch."

Heather, on the other hand, who wed for the second time when she was 40, thought she knew her husband as well as one can know another human being—she met Al at work, dated him for a year, and lived with him for another year before they married. He had a good job with a good company where he was employed for more than ten years, and he was well liked by his supervisors and the other employees. Everything was fine for the first three years of their marriage, then the company downsized and he lost his job.

"That's when things began to fall apart," said Heather. "Al looked for work but couldn't find any because he was in his 50s, and after a while he pretty much gave up. He no longer seems to care about the future.

"I didn't think something like this could happen when we were first together, especially since he seemed so secure in his position," she continued. "He hasn't worked at a steady job for eight years, and he's not even looking anymore. That's what upsets me the most, plus he's racked up a terrible credit rating. My anger toward him for not working for so long has taken its toll on my feelings toward him."

Heather now lives with her daughter in Montana. She said she and Al are friends and stay in touch, but she wants more out of life than what she had with him after the first three years.

"I see no changes, as it stands now," she said. "He's made no effort to look for work. I'm happy I finally got up the strength to stand up for myself and make this change. I would never get married again. I believe marriage is overrated and that most women are happier single."

Say "I Do" Your Way

I remember in the early '50s attending my favorite aunt's wedding—a full-blown, traditional, white-gown church wedding. At the time, I thought her having such an extravagant wedding was really weird. Why? Because she was 42, which to me was ancient and a ridiculous age for a woman to be marching down the aisle in white, just like a young woman. Of course, I was all of 10 or 11, so anyone over 25 was old, as far as I was concerned. But even my mother and some of my other aunts, clucked about her being "a bit long in the tooth" for this kind of wedding.

Fortunately, things have changed and women can have any kind of wedding they want, regardless of age, and no one's going to snicker. You want to wear white and walk down the aisle on the arm of your son, with your grandchildren in attendance? Done. You want a simple wedding on a snowy mountaintop, on cliffs overlooking the ocean, on a ship, in your backyard, at sunrise in a beautiful meadow? Go do it.

Personally, I don't know why anybody would want to put themselves through the stress of a formal wedding, especially if they've been through it once before. After watching my girlfriends suffer the emotional ups and downs of formal weddings when I was in my 20s, I decided when it was my turn, I would elope to Las Vegas. Mother had different ideas, of course, so when I wed for the first time in my early 20s, she and I compromised. I was married in a chapel overlooking the Pacific, near our home in Los Angeles. We had twelve guests in attendance, followed by a brunch in a nearby restaurant—even that was stressful for me. When I married Jerry, about twenty-five years later, we were wed at City Hall in New York, with two close friends in attendance, and then the four of us went off to celebrate with lunch at Windows on the World, atop the World Trade Center. Mother had departed this earth by then, but she would not have approved of an impersonal City Hall wedding. About a month after we were married, Jerry and I hosted a dinner party in a restaurant for a small group of friends and co-workers. But that's just me. I know my type of wedding is in the minority, if the weddings described by many of the Marriage 100 are any indication.

Only 10 were married at City Hall. Of the rest, 39 were wed in a church or synagogue, and nine were married by a justice of the peace in Las Vegas or Reno.

These women did it their way, and not all were conventional about it. When it's your turn, do it your way, because it's probably one of the few times in a woman's life when everyone defers to her wishes—except, perhaps, her mother, if she's still alive. Here's a sprinkling of what some of the brides did to make their special day *very* special.

GEORGIA AND KYLE
A nudist wedding

Perhaps the most unusual wedding was that of Georgia and Kyle, who were married in a nudist colony in central Florida. Georgia is the physical therapist you met earlier (Chapter 4). It was her second wedding, his first. She was 48, he was 41.

"Every winter I'd vacation in Florida and spend some time with friends who owned a nudist colony," said Georgia. "The first time Kyle and I went to Florida together, I took him to the nudist colony to meet my friends. After discovering there was nothing to be nervous about, Kyle really enjoyed the visit and agreed to return the following year.

"He proposed to me at the nudist colony and we decided to be married then and there," she continued. "The next day we held a small, informal ceremony, in the nude, in our friend's living room.

"It's very easy to marry in Florida, there's no residency requirement, no blood test, and a notary public can handle the paperwork." And, in Georgia's case, no clothes to worry about.

Laurel and Daniel
Under the pecan tree

By the third time around, some people start looking for something other than a traditional church wedding. At least that was the case with Laurel and Daniel. She was 40 and he was 50 when they wed, both for the third time.

"We were married Thanksgiving Day, at sunrise in a field under a huge pecan tree near our home in Louisiana," said Laurel. "Six friends were present, it was intimate and extremely romantic."

Maddie and Fred
The whole nine yards, again

For Maddie and Fred, both widowed and marrying for the second time, a large, formal wedding was equally wonderful the second time around, and pretty crowded, too. Between the two of them they have fourteen grown kids and fifteen grandchildren, and every last one of them was involved in the wedding.

"We had a nuptial Mass. All of our children and grandchildren were involved," said Maddie, who was 68 when she rewed. "The children read from the Scriptures, spoke of their hopes and love for us, remembered our deceased spouses. My oldest daughter and Fred's oldest son were our best man and matron of honor. My granddaughter was the altar girl and all the other grandchildren brought gifts for the poor that they offered up at the altar. Then we had a gala reception for seventy family and friends, with dinner and dancing. It was wonderful, as romantic and thrilling as the first time around."

June and Frank
Everyone got into the act

Two others who made it a family affair the second time around were June and Frank. She was 60, he was 59 when they wed. Their combined family totals eight children and fourteen grandchildren, all of whom wanted to get into the act.

"We were married in the same church where we were introduced by his daughter-in-law," said June. "It was a beautiful wedding. I wore an ivory, ankle-length dress with a hat and Frank wore a dark suit. My two oldest daughters were matron and maid of honor and his two oldest sons were their partners. Our grandchildren were bridesmaids and ushers, one of my daughters took the photographs and her husband sang, others took care of the book. No one was left out. After the wedding we had a sit-down dinner for everyone and then Frank and I left for a honeymoon in Hawaii."

ELISE AND JEFF

Shhh, it's a secret

Elise and Jeff, the two travel writers you met earlier, both hate big weddings and planned to elope, sort of.

"We decided not to tell anyone that we were getting married because we both have lots of relatives and if we invited one, we'd have to invite them all," said Elise.

They were married in Chautauqua, an art and cultural center in upstate New York, where Elise was teaching a writing class. Jeff met her there the morning of their wedding with two friends who would stand up for them. They planned to keep it small, just the four of them and the minister, until Elise, who was staying at a boarding house, let it slip over breakfast that she was getting married. Several women at the table were all ears.

"I happened to mention that I was getting married in the afternoon. Four of the women at the table, all in their 70s, got very excited and asked if they could be my bridesmaids. When I said OK, they left and went out searching for flowers," she said.

"Jeff and I were married in a small chapel. I wore a white lace suit that I found in a thrift shop in London that a friend altered for me, and flowers in my hair that the women had gathered," she said. "After the ceremony, as we walked out of the chapel, my 'bridesmaids' blew rainbow-colored soap bubbles at us. The women were lovely and their excitement helped make our wedding very special."

Unfortunately, Elise hadn't made arrangements in time for a special honeymoon suite. The town was packed that week and every room was taken—except for a place that Jeff nicknamed the dungeon.

Later, in a letter to friends and family letting them know of the wedding, Jeff wrote of his honeymoon suite,

"I nicknamed it 'The Dungeon' because the interior was dark, dank, and forbidding, primarily because the 'Dungeon Keeper' kept turning off the light in the dark hallway. The bathroom and shower, with chilly linoleum floors, were at the end of the hall. We spent our wedding night listening to the footsteps of people climbing the stairs above our heads and the complaints of the children in the next room who didn't want to go to bed."

They stayed two nights and then headed home for their new life together, in a house by a lake in upstate New York.

EMILY AND DAVID
A three-day bash

When Emily married David, they decided this would be a wedding every member of their combined families would remember. This includes six kids, six grandchildren, and dozens of aunts, uncles and cousins.

"I wanted our wedding to be a celebration of two people finding the way, and I wanted it to be a family event," she said. "Well, we did it, all right. Our wedding celebration lasted three days and included two hundred guests. We did everything we could think of to make this a memorable occasion, and it was. People are still talking about it."

Emily said she, David, and several family members did all the cooking and preparation themselves. She even baked and decorated her own wedding cake. They also made all the table decorations and favors and helped deck the house and yard with balloons, silk flowers, and ribbons.

"One of the biggest hits was our scavenger hunt," she continued. "We have a large home on seven acres, with a backyard bordering a lake. We set up a tent in the front yard with food and drinks, and in the backyard we cleared paths and created a maze through an area of bushy growth, and then hung more than two hundred items in the bushes and low trees for the scavenger hunt. We paired up small children with older children or adults, gave them lists with fifty different items, and a large bag for holding what they found, and we gave out prizes for the winners.

"We also had boats, canoes and fishing tackles, music and dancing, volleyball, and a tiny wading pool for the little ones. It was, indeed, a wedding to remember," she said.

SUSAN AND LENNY
Our little secret

Susan and Lenny kept their real marriage a big secret for six months and then faked a marriage ceremony aboard a dinner cruise with all their friends and relatives present.

"We were married privately by a justice of the peace in June, but we didn't tell anyone," she said. "In November, we decided to give a party aboard a ship for friends and relatives, and pretend to get married. By now we wanted people to know that we were married, but we were embarrassed to tell them that we had gotten married secretly. We were afraid they'd be angry with us for not telling them."

Susan said they asked the captain of the ship to "marry" them on the dinner cruise.

"It was really just a symbolic marriage because the captain didn't have the legal right to marry us, but nobody knew that," she said. "Just before the wedding the captain asked us for a ring and we realized we'd left our rings at home, so people wouldn't see us enter wearing them. So, we had our little ceremony without the rings, but no one knew the difference, and to this day I have been afraid to tell anyone that we were married long before that shipboard ceremony. It remains our little secret."

Just like these women, you probably have pretty strong ideas about what type of marriage ceremony you want and how you want to handle finances when the honeymoon is over and you return to the daily grind of earning money, balancing checkbooks, and grappling with bills. Splicing together two mindsets, not to mention two incomes, doesn't have to be difficult. Learn from past mistakes and make up your mind to be flexible, and you've got half the battle licked.

Listen Up

Below are a few guidelines offered by the Marriage 100 on how to avoid repeating mistakes concerning both men and money, and how to plan the wedding that's perfect for you:

We can all learn from past mistakes. Just about everyone weighed in on this one. Whether you've been divorced several times or never married but had a string of unhappy relationships, analyze what went wrong, how your expectations differed from the reality of the situation, what you contributed to the anger and hurt. It's not an accident that people tend to repeat the same mistakes—but you don't have to, at least not when it comes to choosing the right man for you. As one woman said, "We can all tell war stories, but why bother. Learn from them and move on."

People rarely change. What you see is what you get. That phrase came up again and again. Be flexible, be realistic, and don't expect perfection were other ways of saying the same thing. A few more thoughts along those lines were,

- "Know what you're getting into and whether you're prepared to make the necessary sacrifices that comprise a marriage."
- "At this age, you're not buying dreams, you're getting reality."
- "You must be ready to close your eyes to imperfections."
- "Don't be rigid in your thinking. Take a second look at the types of men you rejected earlier; you might be surprised to find that their type has grown on you."

Know him well. "Be careful, take your time, update your will," said one woman. "Don't rush," said another. "Know his family, his friends, his co-workers. His relationships with these people will tell you a lot about him." Another said, "Gather as much information as you can on him, know what you're getting into."

Settle money issues before you marry. Money may not necessarily be the root of all evil, but it's certainly the root of a lot of misunderstandings and marital discord. The women were pretty evenly divided on the issue of separate bank accounts. But what they all agreed on was the importance of discussing money issues upfront and deciding in advance how you are going to handle money once you're married. And if he's been married before, don't forget the kids and ex-wives. Like it or not, they're part of the equation. As one woman said, "Be upfront in the beginning, it's very hard to change something once it's in motion."

Follow your heart. Several women said, "Follow your heart," "Trust your instincts," "Do what feels right." After all the practical advice and analyzing, the truth is, you'll probably still go ahead and do what *feels* right. As one said, "I followed my heart and I haven't regretted this marriage for one minute." Another woman said, "I was attracted to husband #1 because he was tall and good looking, to husband #2 because I was lonely and wanted to replace husband

#1, and I married husband #3 because I was so happy to be loved and to give love in return. I've never been happier."

You can elope or have a formal wedding. One of the advantages of being a bride over 40 is you don't have to listen to your mother or your aunts, or anyone else. What you choose to do is your business. If you've dreamed of that formal wedding and missed it the first (or second) time around, do it now. If the first one was a headache you want to avoid, then don't put yourself through that again. Marry in a white gown, or marry in the buff—in a Las Vegas wedding chapel, or in a church or synagogue. It's up to you and don't let anyone tell you differently.

Before you get too complacent and start thinking "Happily ever after," let's take a look at that monkey wrench known as stepchildren and check out the feelings of some of the Marriage 100 on this sometimes touchy subject. Some knew what they were getting into, others didn't. Whether the problem is your kids or his, you'll need to take a cold, hard look at what can happen when you marry and change the family dynamics.

CHAPTER 8

Children: Yours, His, and Theirs

To be willing is only half the task.

—ARMENIAN PROVERB

Bring a new husband into the picture and suddenly the family dynamics change. Even if you're childless, chances are your husband will have children from a former marriage, which means you'll be the one who changes the family dynamics. Some kids will like it, some won't. And don't think that because his children are adults you've nothing to worry about. The children may be grown, with kids of their own, but they can still give you both a lot of headaches.

Eighty-four of the 100 women either had children of their own, or married a man with children and 14 of them had children living at home when they remarried.

Most of the women who became stepmothers admitted they didn't have a clue what they were getting into. Even those who married men whose children lived with their mother, at a supposedly safe distance, invariably ended up with them during vacations, holidays or when the kids had blowups with their mothers. The majority of the women weren't so keen on having to deal with someone else's kids. In many cases, they had their hands full with their own, who weren't thrilled about having a stepfather join the family, let alone those who came with children of their own.

Money was also a big problem. I remember when a friend of mine married a man with two boys. It was her first marriage and his second. She would complain constantly about how much money he was spending on his sons, who were about 10 and 12 at the time and living with their mother 150 miles away.

I often said to her, "Stop complaining, because the way he treats his children from his first marriage is a very good indication of how he'll treat children you may have together. Be thankful you've a husband who loves his kids and takes his responsibilities seriously." That didn't shut her up, unfortunately, but eventually they did have two children of their own, and he's as good to them as he was to his first two.

Many of the Marriage 100 emphasized the importance of observing how a man treats his kids, even if they are grown with children of their own. One of the things I always admired about my husband was his love for his son, an only child. Jerry's son was away at college when we met. He was very generous with him, spending long hours on the telephone giving him advice (rarely heeded, of course), and helping him out financially. While I didn't have children of my own to worry about, I knew that this was a man who took his responsibilities seriously and would always be there for those he loved—and that included me.

PAT
You can never be prepared for this

Pat, the Philadelphia marketing executive who wed for the first time at 40, looks back on her first months with her husband and his daughter and wonders how they got through it. First came her anxiety attacks over giving up her independence, and on the heels of that, she was plunged into stepmotherhood of two teenagers, one who decided to move in permanently.

"A month after I moved in with Pete, his 17-year-old daughter, Jennifer, decided to move in, not for a few days, forever," she said.

That wasn't what Pat bargained for when she sold her house and moved in with Pete. At the time, his two kids, a boy and a girl, were living with their mother in Los Angeles, a safe distance by anyone's standards.

"The children spent summers with Pete and they were with him when we started to date," she said. "I enjoyed them very much, but I also liked the fact that they wouldn't be around all the time. About two weeks before the kids returned to Los Angeles, just before Pete and I were married, I sold my house and moved in with him."

Little did she know that she was to become a full-time stepmother, something she describes as a mixed blessing.

"The kids returned to Los Angeles on schedule, but three weeks later Jennifer called and informed her father that she was coming home—for good," said Pat. "She hated Los Angeles. She'd been out there a year and a half and wanted desperately to be back in Philadelphia at her old high school, with her old friends. What could we say?"

Pat believes she's partly responsible for Jennifer's wanting to stay. "She wanted to be around her dad because, for the first time in many years, she saw him in a very close, loving relationship with someone. I think that made her more comfortable in being around him.

"I was pleased that I'd helped create this type of environment for her, but I was by no means prepared for the double whammy of giving up my single lifestyle *and* being an instant stepmother to a 17-year-old," she said.

"I hadn't lived with anyone for seven years, so here I was, in a period of one month having to get used to living with a man and a teenage girl. I thought, 'Oh my God, how am I going to get through this?'"

Pat warns women who think they are prepared to be stepmothers to think again.

"If you are considering marrying a person with children, especially if this is your first marriage, *really, really* think hard about it," she said. "If I were put in that situation again, I don't know what I would do. It's a lot more stressful than you expect, especially if you've never had children of your own. And I've been fairly lucky—his kids love me, although we've had our problems."

Pat is also convinced that a man with children will always put his children's needs ahead of those of his wife.

"What I learned is that a man's kids are going to come first, and there's not much you can do about it. That's something women need to take a hard look at before they marry a man with children," she said. "What it comes down to is that no matter what you think you know about his kids, no matter how good a relationship you have with your husband and his children, the kids are always in the middle, *always*."

Pat echoes the complaints of many stepparents when she says they are usually cut out of the disciplinary process. In her case, it was a joint decision for her to stay out of it, but she thinks that was a mistake.

"Pete and I decided that I would not discipline his kids, since they were his, not mine," she said. "In retrospect it was a bad decision, even his daughter said so. She threw it back in our faces three weeks after she moved back in, when she told us she didn't know where I fit in the family.

"It's hard to stand by and not get involved when there's a problem," she continued. "Whenever I tried to integrate some of my ideas, I got shot down. That was very difficult for me.

"And then there are the unending 'emergency' phone calls from the ex-wife, frantic because one of the kids is in trouble—and you know, we're three thousand miles away," she said. "His ex-wife called us last spring and said, 'Your son is in trouble, come out here and fix it.' The boy had been caught drinking on school premises and was suspended—let's face it, he was crying for help. We told her we wanted him in counseling, but she refused to do it. The bottom line is, that as the new wife and stepmother, you have very little control over what happens with the kids."

How does a new wife deal with all this? For Pat, the answer lies in one word: communication.

"Pete and I have excellent communication between us," said Pat. "One of the things that I learned from previous relationships is that if you don't talk it out, you can screw things up royally. We've been very honest with each other. Sometimes he agrees with my suggestions concerning his kids, sometimes he disagrees, but we always talk it out and keep the lines open.

"Fortunately, it's eased up a lot because Jennifer is away at college now and is only home for some of the summer months and school holidays. His son stays with us for six to eight weeks in the summer," she said. "We all get along well. They've accepted me as part of the family, and I don't seem to be a problem for them."

Pat said if she has any regrets about marrying late in life, it's that she doesn't have children of her own.

"I would have liked to have a child but, frankly, I wouldn't want to be chasing after a two-year-old when I'm in my late 40s," she said. "I've seen the change in myself between 30 through 35, and I've seen the changes between 35 through 40. I'm not sure I could cope with having a toddler around.

"Just trying to keep up with Pete's kids and their friends when they're visiting is a challenge. I often wonder, 'Could I do it with a two-year-old? And what would I do at 60 with a 15-year-old?' Not a chance."

PAULINE

Check out the kids carefully

Pauline is another one who found out that you're not off the hook just because his kids live with the ex-wife in another part of the country. She's typical of many women who marry men with children and step into a war zone.

"Dealing with my second husband's kids was the most horrible part of my whole life," said Pauline, a divorcee with four young children, who married a man with four children of his own. "No matter where they are, they can still cause tremendous problems. Check out the kids carefully before you consider marrying their father."

When Pauline married Stewart, her children ranged in age from 8 to 14, and his, from 8 to 16.

"I made the mistake of thinking that his kids wouldn't be a problem since they were living with their mother in Chicago and we were in St. Louis. Wrong. It doesn't matter who they're living with, or how many hundreds of miles there might be between you, if they want to make trouble for you and their father, they will," said Pauline. "His oldest son was on drugs and came to live with us for awhile because his mother couldn't handle him anymore. I was a teacher, I thought I could take care of all children, but I found out I couldn't. To make matters worse, my husband always took his children's side when there were arguments. The boy's problems were never resolved, although eventually he went back to his mother. The other three were also troublemakers, but they never lived with us, thank God."

Pauline said it's also important to check out whether his kids are compatible with yours.

"We didn't do that although, thankfully, all the kids did get along well together," she said. "But having his kids around mine a lot really bothered me because their values were very different from what I had instilled in my children. They dropped out of school, they got into drugs, never paid what they owed—real problem kids, not just brats. Fortunately, they didn't influence my kids in any significant way."

When Pauline decided she wanted to remarry, but long before she met Stewart, she got her kids involved by having them make lists of the type of man they wanted for a stepfather.

"I had been divorced from my first husband for about a year when I decided I wanted to remarry," she said. "I hadn't met anyone yet, but I decided it was time to start looking. Before Stewart entered the picture, I asked my children to make a list of the type of stepfather they wanted, so that I could keep their needs in mind when I started dating. I wanted them to have a say in the type of man that would join our family.

"My oldest son wanted someone who was fun and flexible (his father is very stern and rigid), one of my daughters wanted someone who would tell her bedtime stories, and my youngest girl wanted someone who would buy her a horse," she said. "Except for the horse, all of the kids got what they wanted in Stewart. They liked him from day one and they've always had a good relationship with him. I'm the only one who had a problem and that was because of his kids. Maybe I should have made a list of the type of stepchildren I wanted."

TERRY

Watch out for troubled kids and angry ex-wives

When you both have children, and there's a divorce or two out there, there's a good chance at least one of you will end up with a troubled child or an angry ex. Balancing everyone's needs, dealing with ex-wives, forming a new family unit, and all the while staying calm and collected calls for the balancing skills of a Flying Wallenda and the diplomacy of a peace negotiator.

"I'm Ed's third wife. When I married him I had three teenagers at home, and Ed had a four-year-old daughter who lived with his first wife eight hundred miles away, and a two-year-old son who lived with his second wife about ten miles away," Terry said.

When she started dating Ed, Terry was coping with a daughter's alcoholism and drug abuse.

"My daughter was a full-fledged alcoholic at 15," she said, adding that she eventually made the painful decision to have her committed to a treatment center.

"She was there for eight months. Her father wouldn't visit her, but Ed would. She told Ed she hated him and made me promise I wouldn't marry him. I couldn't promise that, but what I did promise was that I wouldn't marry Ed until she was sober and felt better about him.

"This was not an easy situation for a man to walk into, but Ed was very supportive, and he even went into family therapy with us," she continued. "He knew it was important to me and that he was helping save a life. He understood that we couldn't marry until she was sober and in control of her life."

A year later they did marry, with the blessings of all three of Terry's children. Terry said that Ed took easily to the parenting role and was wonderful with all of her kids. But she admits it was difficult at first because of their trying to combine two families.

"My son and two daughters lived with us. His son, a toddler from his second marriage, spent weekends with us," she said. "We worked very hard at trying to be a family and we got through it, but it was rocky at times."

Just before they wed, they sold their individual homes (they both had condos, you'll recall) and bought a house together, something she strongly recommends, if you can afford it.

"We wanted our kids to understand that we were forming a new family unit and we felt we could do this best on virgin territory," she said. "Fortunately, all our kids liked each other and got along well. We didn't see much of his daughter from his first marriage because her mother was vindictive and wouldn't send her for visits or let him see her. His ex even returned all his cards and gifts unopened. I didn't get to know his daughter until she turned 16 and was finally allowed to visit us. Today she has children of her own and we're very close."

All was not well with Ed's second ex-wife, either. She began to make trouble for Terry and Ed about a year into their marriage.

"She started to use their son to blackmail him," she said. "She told Ed that if he didn't give her extra money he couldn't see their son on weekends. Ed would cave in every time. It infuriated me. It took me about a year to see the game that was being played, and when I did, I told him, 'Next time she calls to hold you up, and she says you can't have Bobby, say, fine.' He was reluctant to do it, but at my urging he finally did and it infuriated his ex-wife.

"The standoff lasted six weeks and ended when she called, begging him to take the child for the weekend," said Terry. "I knew it would happen because I know how difficult it is to not be able to get away from your children once in a while.

"If you think ex-wives or stepchildren are playing games, don't be afraid to step in and try to resolve things. After all, you have a stake in it too," she said.

LENORE
Find someone without kids

"Thank God he didn't have any children. I had enough on my hands with my own kids. I'm not sure I would have married someone with children."

Lenore's the one with three daughters you met earlier. Her daughters were ages 9 to 17 when she married Jake, the bachelor.

"Jake is very good with children. He has three nieces that he's very close to, and he got along well with my kids from day one," she said.

Like Pat, her biggest problem with her spouse was in methods of discipline, only this time it was Lenore who insisted on being the sole disciplinarian.

"He wanted to be the disciplinarian, but I said no, they're my children," she said. "Our styles of parenting are very different. I trust my daughters and my attitude toward them is, if I haven't reared them with proper values, they aren't going to change now. His style is more rigid. He's less willing to look at things developmentally, to realize that most of the problems with kids are just stages they go through in their development. If he had children of his own, it would have been much more difficult for me. I know I would have had trouble treating all the kids alike."

Even though he wasn't allowed to discipline them, Jake helped the girls in different, equally important ways—he gave them the male point of view about things that concerned them, and that was very important to them.

"When we married, my youngest had a self-confidence problem. She was convinced that none of the kids liked her," said Lenore. "Nothing I or her sisters said to reassure her made any difference. I just couldn't get through to her. But Jake had long talks alone with her and got through to her. He was able to instill confidence in her. I really appreciated that. I guess she needed to hear it from a man. She adores him, they all do."

LINDA
Give them time

Sometimes the kids dislike your new husband because they resent his intrusion into the family, and other times because they feel that liking their stepfather means being disloyal to their father. Linda's advice is to take it easy, give them time to get to know each other and hope for the best. Linda, if you'll recall, was the divorcee with four children who met her husband, Don, at a ski resort.

"I was very young when I had my children and only one was still living at home when I started dating Don," she said. "It was very important to me that all of my kids approve of him.

"If my second husband were someone my children didn't like, I think it would be very difficult for me to have a good marriage, even if the kids were grown and out of the house. I would be constantly trying to defend him to my kids or feel uncomfortable at the family gatherings," she continued. "You don't want your children to run your life, but you do want to take their feelings into account."

Linda admits it wasn't smooth sailing at first. When she started dating Don, all of her kids gave her a hard time, even the three who no longer lived at home.

"My ex-husband was terminally ill," she said. "I think the kids were torn and were feeling a little bit like, 'Oh, here's mom, she's divorced and running all over the world with a new boyfriend. She has this great life, while dad is pining for her and literally losing his life.'

"Even though they didn't have anything concrete against Don, they were uneasy about the relationship. They thought their liking Don was being disloyal to their father," she said. "They had nothing concrete to criticize. They couldn't say this guy is an alcoholic, or anything equally obvious. They just were prepared not to like him.

"My oldest daughter, who was married and living in Ohio at the time, referred to him as 'that Don person,' even though she had never met him. Before we were married, I took Don to Ohio to meet her and I was very upset by her behavior—she was a cold, obnoxious bitch. She didn't even know this man, yet she was a snot to him because I was enjoying this nice life with him," she said. "Luckily, the more they were around Don, the more my kids warmed up to him. By the time we were married, they were happy about it.

"One of the reasons I got married again was that I still had a 12-year-old son at home, and I felt he needed a stable family life," she continued. "When my ex-husband became ill, the job of raising our son landed completely on my shoulders, and I thought this 'Swinging Singles Scene' is not a good life for the mother of a young boy. With Don, I was able to settle down again with one man and create a family environment. For me, that's the major reward in this marriage. My son's a super kid. I often wonder if I had gone the other route, never settling down, what he'd be like today."

CANDICE
Let 'em pout

Although Candice only has one child, he was every bit as difficult as Linda's four when she brought a new man into her life, except she didn't care because he was old enough to be on his own.

"My son, Jim, was almost 18 when I started dating Art," she said. "I divorced his father when Jim was four and he disappeared from our lives. Jim was used to having me to himself and hated any man I dated. My son's an artist and a loner. He and I had developed a closeness and friendship through the years, respecting each other's privacy. He had his space and I had mine. I'm sure he felt that somebody else coming into the picture would ruin this comfy life of his."

Like Linda, she met her husband at a ski resort, but she wasn't alone, she was with her son, her parents, and her sister.

"Art and I met on the slopes where I was giving my dad skiing lessons. Later we all went to dinner together, the whole family, including my son," she said. "Everyone liked Art except my son."

Despite Jim's displeasure, Candice started dating Art right away, and a few months later Art moved in with them.

"Jim pouted a lot when Art was around and stared daggers at him. It really annoyed me," she said. "One night I said to him, 'You're 18, you're not stupid, it's time to get reality here.' Eventually he got used to it," she said. "I would never have had a man move in with me if I had young children at home, but at 18 they should be old enough to let their mother have a life."

Candice credits her mother for helping straighten out her son. "She asked him, 'Would you like to take care of your mother when she's old?' My son, who has a fair amount of intelligence, thought about this, decided the answer was no, and started to come around."

Straightening out Art was next. Candice took a no-nonsense approach when Art started grumbling about Jim's attitude toward him and what he considered Jim's bad manners.

"I told him to stay out of it, that Jim is my son, I raised him. I said, 'If you don't like the way he behaves, I can't help it. It's none of your business. Whatever's wrong with him, it's too late for you to fix it,'" she said. "It took a couple of years, but they both finally came around and now they're friends." Jim went away to college shortly after that, which probably didn't hurt either.

Art has a grown daughter from his first marriage, but Candice said the relationship between him and his ex-wife was strained and he saw very little of his daughter when she was growing up.

"Now she's married with a child of her own," said Candice. "We get along just fine but her relationship with her father is still tense. I'm hoping they'll be able to enjoy each other someday, but I stay out of it."

ALICE

Keep your mouth shut

When you marry a man with young children who live with their mother, you'll probably have to deal with a man who feels guilty about leaving his kids. And, there's a good chance that his kids (not to mention ex-wife) know how to use this guilt to their advantage. For Alice, there's a balancing act in knowing when to speak up and when to keep quiet.

"This is my fifth marriage and my fourth experience at being a stepmother. What have I learned? Keep your mouth shut about things that are not so important. Save it for the really important issues, like money. If you get involved in the small issues, you get a name for being meddlesome and always talking about problems. Save the mouth for the big ones."

When Alice married Brad, the father of three teenagers, she was 51 (you met her in Chapter 4). Her two daughters were grown and long gone by then, but his three were living with their mother a few miles away.

"The three most frequently uttered words of a divorced man with children are, 'I feel guilty,'" she said. "Brad has an incredible inability to say no to his children whenever they ask for more—even when he knows they're being selfish," she said. "And don't think that once they've come of age that the money requests stop. His kids are on their own now, with very good jobs and earning more than he ever did, but still they play on his guilt and hint about needing more. It never ends.

"Money can be an especially big problem for both of you if his kids are not yet of age," she said. "Brad always gave his children extra money, over and above the settlement agreement.

"You have to be upfront about money from the beginning," she continued. "If you complain later and tell him he spends too much on his kids, you'll look grabby, selfish and self-serving. The kids will pick up on that and play it back, no matter what their age."

Like Pat, Alice believes that a man with children is always going to put his kids ahead of his new wife.

"When it comes right down to it, your husband is going to put his kids first, so always put aside money for yourself," she said. "You have to protect yourself financially because, through guilt, more likely than not, he's going to spend his money on his children before he's going to spend it on you. Protect yourself by having a separate bank account for yourself. But don't be sneaky, be upfront about it."

Alice believes strongly that it's very important to establish rules in the beginning of a relationship, and it's especially important when it comes to stepchildren and money.

"Tell him, 'This is what I'm doing and why,' with the implication that if he doesn't like it, that's going to have to be his problem," she said. "It's equally important if you also have children from previous marriages. You must set up rules in advance, so there is absolutely no misunderstanding when they start coming around, hat in hand."

Alice also cautions against making negative comments about ex-wives.

"Don't criticize his ex-wife," she said. "I never did that, but I've seen it happen with others. You don't have to be friendly with them if you don't want to, but you should have a polite arrangement, if possible. It's important, because if you make nasty comments, all you do is put your husband on the defensive, even if he agrees with you. His ex-wife is, after all, the mother of his children.

"If she calls, talk to her in a casual tone of voice. Otherwise, it gets back to him that you're being bitchy. Even if you don't like her, strive for a good relationship, because if she feels negative toward you, she's going to lay it on the kids—they're going to feel awkward when you're around, your husband is going to be defensive, and you're letting yourself in for a lot of problems you don't need."

Cassie
Come in on little cat feet

When Cassie, whom you met in Chapter 5, wed for the second time at 47, both her son and her husband's three daughters were grown and on their own. She has few complaints about being a stepmother, but she does caution women to enter gently into any new family, or risk rejection. To paraphrase Carl Sandburg, the poet, be like the fog that comes in on little cat feet, sit on silent haunches, and observe.

"You have to tread lightly and try to understand his children, and you must give them time to get to know you before you marry," she said. "It's sort of like being a mother-in-law. You must be careful what you say to them and how you say it. See your stepchildren as people, don't try to force your ideas on them or expect them to understand the way you do things.

"I was very fortunate that my stepchildren were adults when I married Steve," she said, adding that, in her case, she was marrying into a family with a very different background from her own. She's Jewish, urban born and raised, he's Protestant and has lived most of his life in the suburbs. He was a widower twelve years her senior, who had been married for thirty-four years. She was a divorcee and single mom.

Cassie said the two youngest daughters accepted their father's remarriage, but the oldest one had some problems with it.

"Steve didn't talk a lot about his personal life to his daughters, which is typical of men of his generation," she said. "He'd have casual conversations with them and once, maybe he mentioned he was dating, but they had no clue he was serious about anyone. One day he said to his oldest daughter, who was living in Detroit, 'Oh, by the way, I'm getting married.' There she was, a thousand miles away and she didn't have a clue what was going on.

"I suggested we visit her and let her get to know me before we married," said Cassie. "I told Steve that if she didn't like me, there wasn't much we can do about it, but I felt we should at least give her a chance to get to know me. You have to put the right foot forward, because if you get off on the wrong foot with your stepchildren, you'll probably never enjoy a good relationship with them.

"I tried very hard to figure out, 'What are they thinking? What's the best way to present our marriage plans to them?' I didn't want to meet his family with the attitude of, 'This is what we're going to do and you have to take it or leave it,'" she said.

Although the meeting with Steve's daughter was pleasant and polite, it wasn't until after she and Steve were married that his daughter warmed up to her.

"Two years after we were married, we visited her again," she said. "We started talking and all of a sudden we found we were thinking along the same lines. Her husband said to me, 'You really love this guy, don't you? You know he's pretty strait-laced and conservative.' I told him, 'Yes, I know he is, but there are facets to him you haven't seen.' Later, his daughter said to me, 'It's so nice to see my father happy and enjoying his life.' That comment really touched my heart."

ANNETTE
Be a favorite aunt

Annette, the writer who married her former boss, had a loving relationship with her stepchildren long before she became romantically involved with their father. During the twelve years she worked for Marv, the children often came to her for advice and she became their friend and confidant.

"One thing that really impressed me about Marv was how involved he was with his children," she said. "When things went wrong, they called him at the office and he'd have long talks with them. A lot of times he'd ask for my advice. Now, I've never had children but I do have strong opinions about how to raise them and I'm not shy about stating what's on my mind."

She said some of her advice really pleased the kids, such as the time Marv complained about their being on the phone at home all the time, tying up the line.

"He was always complaining about his kids tying up the phone and how clients couldn't get through," she said. "I told him, 'Get a separate phone line for them and you won't have that problem.' He did and they loved me for it." Over the years she had lots of good, common sense advice that made the kids happy and they developed a very strong bond with her.

"I watched them grow up," she said. "I was like a favorite aunt to them. As they entered their teens, they sometimes came to me for advice and confided things to me that they didn't want to discuss with their parents.

"By the time Marv and I were romantically involved they were in college," she said. "When they heard we were going to get married, their first question was, 'What if it doesn't work out? Will you still be our friend?' I was very touched by that."

Annette said that despite their close relationship with her, there were some problems with the kids in the beginning of her marriage.

"They were concerned because whenever they saw Marv, they saw me, too," she continued. "They complained that they had no private time with their father. After that I made him schedule dates with his children for times when I wouldn't be around. And you know what? Eventually they stopped wanting those private times.

"I knew I was a full-fledged member of the family the day they had a family conference and they said to me, 'You can't go off in the kitchen, you're a part of this family now, you have to listen to this, too.'"

Annette said she also knew she had made it when a son who lives in San Diego started addressing his letters home, "Dear Dad and Annette" instead of "Dear Dad."

Although not everyone can have the type of relationship Annette had through the years with her stepchildren, she does believe you should get to know your husband's children as soon as possible. "Your marriage mustn't come as a surprise, you want them to feel comfortable having you around."

And while you're waiting for that special man and his children to show up, here are some wise words from Annette:

"If you love children, but feel it's too late to have any of your own, bring other people's children into your life. I've never had a sense of loss over not having children because I am involved with nine nieces and nephews and many of my friends' children. I've been to hundreds of weddings, christenings and bar mitzvahs. Enjoy other people's kids; it's good training—if you marry a man with children, you'll be ready for them."

MAGGIE
You'd better like children

"There are bound to be difficulties with stepchildren," said Maggie, a divorcee who, at 55, wed a 44-year-old widower with two small children at home.

"My two sons were already married when I married Tom, who had a son and daughter just entering their teens," she said. "It's very important that you like children to begin with, and that you try to understand his children, no matter what their age. If you don't, you should not marry a man with young children, especially if they live with him. It will lead to heartache for all concerned."

Maggie, a secretary, quit her job shortly after she remarried to take care of her two stepchildren.

"I was single for eighteen years before I met Tom. Suddenly being a mother of young children again was quite a challenge," she said.

"Basically, I enjoyed it, but I always felt I had to make sure I did the right thing, that I wasn't allowed to make mistakes. Eventually I realized I was the only one putting that kind of pressure on myself, that no one was expecting perfection of me. It took about six months, but after that I began to think of them as my own children. Now they're grown and on their own, but I'm still mom."

MARY

Wait till the kids are grown

Mary thinks it's a good idea to wait until your kids are grown before you consider remarriage. A single mom who wed for the second time at 46, after the kids were on their own, she said she was steered away from remarriage by ugly newspaper accounts and TV programs about painful relationships between stepparents and stepchildren.

"Even though I know the media plays up the worst-case scenarios, I didn't want to risk putting myself and my kids through any grief, or having someone else's children interfere with my relationship with my own children," she said.

Mary said she felt really lucky that she met her husband, Ray, after her kids left home. He was twice-divorced, with four children from his first marriage and three stepchildren from his second marriage that he loves as much as his own.

"Ray adores my children. He's very good to them, like the father they never had," she said. "We have twelve grandchildren between us," she said. "They're all part of our family and everyone gets along well. There's no animosity, no conflict, nothing ugly going on between family members. We're very lucky. I wonder if we would have been such a harmonious family if Ray and I had met earlier when our kids were young."

APRIL

Don't force a relationship

April has a comfortable relationship with her grown stepchildren—now—but things got off to a rocky start when she thought they could all be one warm, happy family. It didn't work.

"If you both have grown children when you marry, it's better not to try to mix them," said April, a widow with three children who, at 64, wed a man with two children.

"Having one big, happy family sounds nice, but it's rare. At first I tried getting more involved with Peter's children, but it just didn't work out the way I hoped it would," she said. "Finally, I let go and decided that it was better to let things work out naturally, not to try to influence or push them in any direction. If you try too hard, it just opens the door for more conflict.

"I have a wonderful relationship with my daughter and when I first married Peter, I wanted to have the same type of relationship with his daughter, do some of the same things together. I set up some lunch dates, but they were very awkward. Not that his daughter isn't a likeable person, I was just pushing too hard," said April. "I wanted all of Peter's kids and their spouses to like me and I went out of my way to be their friend, but the more I tried, the more they pulled back. It was the wrong thing to do.

"What I learned is, if your children are grown, put your relationship with your husband first," she said. "Your children and stepchildren have their own lives to live and you have yours, and that's the way it should be. Even with my daughter, as close as we are, I let her know my husband comes first—it works better that way. Both sides of the family are now on very friendly terms and we are usually together on holidays. We're not as close-knit as I would like, but I've accepted it."

JO
Don't expect too much

Therapists have as much trouble with stepchildren as other women, judging from conversations Jo has had with her therapist. She went for some advice about her relationship with her stepchildren and found out the therapist shared some of her concerns. Jo, if you'll recall, has no children, but married a man with three grown children.

"I always wanted to marry a man with grown children, not small ones, because I never wanted to raise kids," said Jo. "I think that melding two sets of children is very, very difficult. I would never want to try it.

"My therapist told me that having stepchildren is never really going to be what people think. She herself thought she could have this really close relationship with her stepson, and it never was," said Jo. "There are too many negative feelings on the part of so many stepchildren. Often they're angry at their parents for divorcing, or they're angry at their father for something he did twenty years ago. These things have nothing to do with you, but if they're not dealt with by their father (and they usually aren't), they get projected onto you. It doesn't mean that it's going to be terrible, it just means that it's not going to be as good as you want it to be.

"After talking to my therapist, I realized my relationship with my stepchildren is pretty typical," she said. "I wanted to have a really close relationship, but it's not, and I've accepted it. That's not to say it can't happen, but it's not something to expect."

RUTH
Beware the minefield of resentments

Ruth, now in her third marriage, felt that she spent her second marriage tiptoeing through minefields after she and her ex-husband combined two sets of kids that were about the same age. She warns women to think twice about setting up a household with his and her children.

"My second marriage was fraught with difficulties because we put two families of children together," said Ruth, adding that her third marriage is (happily) childless. "In my second marriage, I had four children, two boys and two girls, ranging in age from 5 to 12; he had a son, 8, and a daughter, 10. They all lived with us, and somehow we managed to stay together for sixteen years even though it was turbulent.

"But when the last kid left home, all the resentments that had built up over the years, mostly related to the children, burst forth and there wasn't much to salvage of our relationship. We split up. I would not blame the failure of the marriage totally on the children, but they certainly had a part in it. It's very, very difficult to combine two sets of children. I would not recommend it."

Ruth was 56 when she wed for the third time, to a 56-year-old widower with a grown son: "None of them live with or near us—that's the best part."

IRIS AND KAREN
You don't need their approval

One of the advantages of older marriages is that you can forget about your kids' needs and concentrate on your own, and the older you get, the easier it gets. At least that's how two widows, whom you've met earlier, feel. One is Iris, mother of one, who remarried at 63. The other is Karen, mother of four, who rewed at 67.

"We were married quietly at City Hall because neither of us wanted to go through a big wedding again," said Iris. "We didn't tell our kids until a month later. It wasn't because we were afraid they wouldn't approve, it made no difference to us whether they approved or not. Besides, we had been living together for eight months, so it wasn't as if there was going to be a drastic change in our lifestyle. You have to do what you're comfortable with. You let your kids live their own lives, they should let you live yours.

Iris's husband, Michael, has two sons, both married and in their 40s. "We decided to tell them when my daughter came to visit from California. His kids were living nearby and we invited them all out to dinner. My daughter was ready to wring my neck—not because she was unhappy about the marriage, but because I kept it a secret from her. They were all very surprised, but happy for us."

Karen and her husband, Jack, who have six kids and twelve grandchildren between them, kept their relationship quiet for a couple months, not only from their children, but everyone.

"I didn't tell the kids right away because I felt it was none of their business," she said.

They announced their marriage plans to all their kids over a Thanksgiving dinner.

"Their jaws dropped, practically in unison," she said. "Some of my grandchildren felt that I wasn't being sufficiently loyal to their grandfather, little knowing that my remarrying was exactly what he had wanted. But they all came around once they got over the shock."

Karen and Jack had a small church wedding, with her oldest son giving her away, two granddaughters by her side as bridesmaids, and Jack's son acting as best man.

"We've never had any problems as stepparents," she said. "Jack and I did what my first husband and I did, which is marvelous if you can afford it—we take grandchildren abroad, in small batches. I told Jack about it, and he thought it was a great idea. We took his two grandsons to Europe last year. They were in their teens. It was great fun for all of us, and it really helped link me into the family circuit.

Money: Yours, His, and Theirs

If you don't think money (read, inheritance) doesn't play a big role in how happy his kids are to see you marry their father, or how happy your kids are to welcome him into the family, guess again.

Where grown kids are involved, the burning issues all seem to stem from the M (for Money) word or the I (for inheritance) word.

Should you sign a prenuptial agreement, make out a will in advance of your marriage, leave everything to each other, and let the kids, if they're grown, fend for themselves? Whatever you do, someone will probably be unhappy about it.

Perhaps the potential for problems is best summed up by Hilda, who at 54 wed Ben, 59. She has one grown child, he has two.

"His children felt threatened by our marriage because my husband is well-off and they were afraid that they'd lose part of their inheritance," she said. "To them, I wasn't someone who had joined the family and was making a nice home for their father, I was someone who might cheat them out of their inheritance."

My personal favorite is this comment from Doris, who wed for the first time at 45, "Neither of us have children, but his nieces and nephews were not happy to see us marry because they were afraid his will would be rewritten to exclude them. And it was."

Just about everyone had a strong opinion about how money and inheritance issues affected their relationship with their stepchildren, and how it affected their own kids' feelings about their new stepfather.

Prenuptials: Pros and Cons

It's apparently not just the super-rich who sign prenuptials. A lot of women in this survey signed them and believe strongly in them. Many others did not and are staunchly against them. Those who are against them ask, "Where's the trust?" Many who are for them say, "Prove you're not marrying for money," or "Do it to protect your assets and your kids." Here's a sampling of opinions from some of the women—you've already met several of them:

Delia, mother of two: "I think prenuptials only serve the person with the most amount of money and the highest income, which is usually the man. My husband and I both have two adult children. In our wills, we leave everything to each other. If we go together, the money is split down the middle between our two sets of kids. If your adult children or stepchildren dislike you because they see you as an enemy who'll take away their inheritance, that's too bad. Who needs people like that around? It's different, of course, if the kids are young and still financially dependent. Then, and only then, do you each have a moral obligation to see that they're provided for."

Marlene, mother of two: "Don't sign a prenuptial (I call it an antinuptial) agreement. It's like worrying about divorce before you're even married and putting yourself on probation. If you feel it necessary to sign one, make sure the probation period only lasts three years. You must have a strong voice in how money is distributed; it must be a real partnership, otherwise the marriage is not going to move forward smoothly and equitably."

Karen, mother of four: "I'd definitely recommend a prenuptial, even if you don't have children. Your money should stay in your family and his should stay in his, even it if goes to nieces and nephews. A prenuptial clears the air and demonstrates that no one has ulterior motives."

Emily, mother of three: "Prenuptials? Absolutely not! It's a question of trust. A prenuptial says you're going into a marriage figuring it won't work. To protect your kids? There are better ways to protect them. We've put everything in a trust—what's mine goes to my kids, what's his, goes to his kids."

Alex, mother of two: "We don't have a prenuptial. I think they're OK, but I think a will is more important, because it defines what the children of each of you inherits. I thought about this recently because of some property that I bought and developed before I was married. I knew if I went first, my husband would own that property and he'd eventually will it to his children. My daughters wouldn't see a penny from it, even though I knocked myself out to get it. I rewrote my will to be certain that property ends up with my daughters, not his children. This is something I should have thought of before I remarried. If you do things after the fact, it's terribly hard to go backwards and clean up the mess. Try to do it later and you end up with the automatic, 'Why don't you trust me?' Luckily, in this case, there was no problem."

Terry, mother of three: "Although we don't have a prenuptial, I do believe in them. It means that both partners stand on equal footing. If both partners have an income, they should be willing to spell things out so there are no misunderstandings. If a woman with a much lower income than her husband signs a prenuptial, what's she going to lose? Something she never had in the first place. Unless, of course, she's marrying for money."

Irene, mother of two: "I definitely believe in having a prenuptial because it clears the air. His three children weren't pleased about our marriage because they were worried about their inheritance. One son, in particular, detested me—he was afraid of losing money he was counting on. Once he found out about our prenuptial, he calmed down and started being nice to me. I don't really blame the kids who worry about their inheritance. I've seen too many cases where a man remarries and the adult children of his new wife come in and wipe him out."

Elise, mother of three: "I have very few assets, but I wanted a prenuptial so his kids wouldn't think I was a gold digger. My husband was against it, so we don't have one. At my insistence, we had wills drawn up after we were married that outline whose kids get what. It was a concern of mine, but no one else seemed to care. He has two grown sons and from everything that I can see, they are happy to see their father happily married again and aren't looking for money from him. We're lucky that way."

If you're contemplating marrying a man with children and feel you need some help in learning to cope with his kids or in blending families, a good place to start is the Stepfamily Association of America (SAA). A nonprofit organization, it has chapters throughout the country and acts as a clearinghouse and referral agency for resources available to stepparents. You can reach them at 650 J St. Suite 205, Lincoln, NE 68508; tel. 1-800-735-0329, or 402-477-7837.

Listen Up

The bottom line, whether it's kids or prenuptials, is you can never be too careful or know enough about a man or his family. Along those lines, the Marriage 100 offer some more time-honored advice and a mix of insights on stepparenting and blending families, and how to do it with the least amount of grief.

Watch how he treats his family. Practically all the women said they couldn't respect a man who wasn't good to his kids, but many said watch out if his children always have their hands out. "Observe how freely he gives money and expensive gifts to his children. If he goes overboard, it's an indication that something's wrong," said one woman. Another said, "Get to know his children and his friends before you get too involved; they tell you a lot about a man." "How he treats his children and grandchildren is a prime indication of his character," said another.

Grown kids can be just as difficult. Many women, especially those who've never had children, think that because a man's children are grown and out of the house that they won't be much of a problem. Think again. According to many of the Marriage 100, grown children can be as demanding as the younger ones. "Age doesn't make any difference. They can give you just as hard a time when they're 30 as they can when they're 13," said a mother of two who married a man with four children, all grown. Another said, "You are marrying him and his family—especially the kids, it doesn't matter what age they are." Another warned, "They always have their hand out, they never seem to outgrow the need to take."

Stepparenting is stressful. Count on it. Even if his kids live with their mother, they'll probably be around for weekends and holidays. "I married a man with two children, 11 and 12 years old, who spend two weeks out of every month with us. It's been very stressful," said a woman who was in her first marriage. Another said, "I was warned by a friend that being a stepmother isn't worth the aggravation. She was right. I wish I'd listened to her." "I'm not close to my husband's children; they're very draining—something's always going wrong and it's always someone else's fault, never theirs," said a stepmother of four grown children. "It takes patience, a lot of understanding, so much love, and usually some counseling," said a mother of three, who wed a man with one small child. Said another, "Our marriage blossomed *after* the kids moved out." "Beware your husband's female children," said another, whose stepdaughters are in their 40s and giving her a hard time. "Daughters have more trouble letting go of their fathers than do sons." A woman who wed at 41 summed it all up with, "Think twice about marrying him if there are two sets of children involved and ex-spouses nearby."

Don't surprise them. Although a few of the women said their marriage was nobody's business but their own, most advised against springing it on the kids. It just creates resentment. "From the moment the relationship turns serious, involve your kids so they can get used to the idea of your remarrying. It doesn't matter how old they are, they need to be eased into it," said one woman. Another said, "If he's close to his children and grandchildren, try to involve them in your life. The fewer surprises on both sides, the better."

Meet the entire family. You're marrying the whole family, whether you like it or not. "Watch carefully how he interacts with his family and yours," said one 50-year-old bride. "The children, yours and his, are crucial to your happiness, even if they're grown." Another said, "Get to know his family. If they're a big part of his life, they'll become a big part of your life, whether you like it or not."

Prepare to wear many hats. The older you are, the greater the chance that you'll not only marry a man with children, but also with grandchildren. As one woman said, "In one fell swoop you can become a stepmother, mother-in-law, and grandmother."

Think "our" kids, not "his" and "mine." Most of the women talked about "my" children and "his" children, but one, a mother of two, said, "At first our kids were put off at the idea of our marriage, but things changed dramatically once we adopted an attitude of all the kids being *our* children. It emphasized that we were all family and there were no favorites."

OK, so you've tackled the stepparenting issue and you've decided on whether to sign a prenuptial—now let's try to glimpse the future and see what that important first year of marriage often brings. According to the Marriage 100, a lot of unpleasant issues surface during the first year and it's never too early to start thinking about how to handle them.

CHAPTER 9

The First Year

Even a good marriage is a time of trial.
—ITALIAN PROVERB

Here's what to expect: conflict over money, family, and personal space, not to mention differing tastes in movies, books, travel, and anything else you might have deemed important in your single years.

It's not always easy for two people, used to doing things their own way, to set up a household together. On weekends, maybe he likes to sit in front of the TV and watch sports all day; you may like to go to the movies, or to your health club.

The most common complaint among the women was having less time to themselves, "You tend not to realize how much time a husband can take up in your life," said a 40-year-old bride, an avid reader who no longer has the time to read a lot and regrets it. Another common complaint was, "I'm neat, he's messy," or vice versa (although the neat one was almost always the woman), or, "He saves everything, and it piles up, it drives me nuts but I don't dare touch it."

Many of the women mentioned the need for personal space. One said, "No matter how cramped your living quarters, you and your husband each need a private place to retreat to, to read, or watch TV, or work a crossword puzzle or do whatever you damn well please in peace and quiet." Another wanted space "to just sit and listen to the glorious silence."

Conflicting points of view also cause trouble: "Our fiercest battles were over politics. He's Republican, I'm Democrat—now that's the real definition of a mixed marriage," said Cassie, the Jewish divorcee whose second husband is a church-going Episcopalian.

STELLA
Don't raise the toilet seat issue

If comments from the Marriage 100 are any indication, the world is full of messy, sloppy, don't-throw-anything-out-types of men who somehow seem to link up with neat and organized women. Stella, the school teacher who married for the second time at 47, thinks this is all trivial stuff and cautions women about making a big deal of it.

He leaves the toilet seat up? Towels on the floor? So what. Forget it. That's Stella's advice.

"There will always be petty challenges, especially in your first year," she said. "You're neat and well organized, he's not. He leaves the toilet seat up, or forgets to put the cap on the toothpaste tube and, God forbid, squeezes the tube from the middle. Or he tosses wet towels on the floor, doesn't hang up his clothes—all these things may be annoying, but they're not really important in the long run. You can work around them.

"When I lived alone, nothing was out of order. Well, that all changed in my first year with Carl," she continued. "I won't say it was easy, but my priority is my marriage, not a spotless house. One of the things you must do in any relationship is learn to compromise and to keep your priorities straight.

"If he leaves his clothes on the floor, or the empty soda cans on the coffee table, don't nag him about it, just pick them up and go on with your life. It only takes a few minutes, a lot less time than it takes to argue about it," she said. "He's not going to change and it's just not worth getting upset over it. This doesn't mean you're going to be his maid, it just means you have to overlook some of his bad habits, or you're always going to be angry and upset, and it's simply not worth it."

JOYCE
Ignore his idiosyncracies

Joyce has much the same attitude as Stella, except that her problem isn't that her husband is messy, it's that he's too neat. He's obsessively neat, according to Joyce. But, like Stella, she's got her priorities straight and is focused on his good traits.

"My husband is extremely neat; I am not," she said. "When my sister met Ken, she told everyone, 'This marriage isn't going to last because Joyce could never live with a man who folds paper bags and then stacks them all facing the same direction.'"

Even Joyce admits it was a challenge in the beginning, "I just decided early on to keep my mouth shut and be tolerant of his idiosyncracies, and I advise all women to do the same. Nobody's going to change. What you see is what you get. Focus on what's important—tell him every day how much he means to you, how wonderful he is, how much you love him. That's what counts."

JUDY
Do your own thing

Women who've been career-driven and independent most of their lives sometimes find it difficult to socialize with the homebody wives of their husband's friends and business associates.

Judy, the school guidance counselor who wed for the first time at 44, is a good example of that. She said her biggest adjustment in her first year of marriage was finding herself in social situations where she was expected to join the women, when what she really wanted was to be with the men. Her husband, George, is an amateur photographer, and in the first few months of their marriage he would take her to meetings of a photography club he belonged to, where everybody brought their wives. The trouble was, from her point of view, all the wives were mothers and full-time homemakers. She had nothing in common with them and was thoroughly bored with their conversation and frustrated because she wasn't used to situations where the sexes were separated.

"When I first went to a meeting of his club, I found all the wives sitting in one corner, and all the men in another corner. A lot of the men were in education and there was a fair amount of shop talk going on," she said. "Things were being said that interested me and I wanted to join in, but I knew I would be resented if I did, by both groups.

"I was used to being in charge or working with whoever was in charge of a situation, of conducting meetings, of speaking my mind," she continued. "At these meetings, I kept my mouth shut and stayed with the wives, but I didn't like it. I'm not putting down women or 'women's talk,' which often is more interesting than what men have to say. But this particular group of women were not women I had anything in common with. Their interests revolved around home and family, and that's OK, but I had absolutely nothing to add to their conversations. After a few months, I stopped going and let George go without me. He didn't mind one bit, and no one seemed to care."

Judy looks at this as an example of the learning process and adjustment phase of any new marriage—finding out what things they like to do together and what they prefer to let the other partner do alone. She bowed out of the photo club meetings with no hard feelings, and George, on the other hand, bowed out of one of her great loves, bridge. Now she goes off to her bridge parties alone and he goes off to his photo club alone, and both couldn't be happier with the arrangement.

"We share just about every other interest—travel, books, TV shows, and the fun of just puttering around the house together," she said.

PEGGY
Make him talk things out

Having open lines of communication is crucial to the success of any relationship, but especially important in the early stages of a marriage. Peggy, the woman who wed the train conductor at 40, said she had to work very hard the first year to get her husband to express his feelings to her.

"Our first year was very difficult," said Peggy. "I had a lot of trouble getting Ian to talk and open up; it was very hard. If I told him I didn't like something he did or was upset about something that involved him, he often felt very intimidated. It would upset him and he'd dummy up. During our first year, I had to constantly reassure him that just because I cried or yelled at him, it didn't mean I didn't love him or that his opinions weren't worthwhile. He took everything personally.

"It took me a few months so see the light, but I realized that I had to change my attitude," she continued. "He didn't expect me to change, so why should I expect him to change? I learned to relax and not get angry so often. I simply became more accepting of his shortcomings, and why not? He was always very accepting of mine."

LOIS
Give it time

"At the beginning I noticed that I wasn't used to sharing—or even sleeping a full night with anyone," said Lois, the dating service reject who wed for the first time at 44. "Learning to live with a man when you're used to being alone takes a lot out of you, especially if you marry for the first time in your 40s.

"I had never lived with a man until I moved in with Charles, and then it was only after we became engaged," she continued. "Years before, I was in a relationship where I'd go to my boyfriend's apartment, sometimes spend the night and leave the next morning, but it really wasn't the same as living full time with someone. I always had my own place to return to, my own space and privacy, and that was very important to me.

"After Charles and I moved into a condo together, I developed a very bad cold, which I'm sure was brought on by stress," she continued. "Even though I felt fortunate in having found someone like him, it was hard learning to share the space. The first few months can be stressful, but as you move forward in a marriage, you adjust and the anxieties melt away."

GERRY

Demand your own time and space

"After ten years of being single following my first marriage, I found living with someone again very, very difficult," said Gerry, the secretary who wed for the second time at 45. "During those ten years I went from being a passive person to being assertive. I got used to taking care of myself and I liked it that way. My husband is more the dependent type than I am. He needs to be taken care of, especially when it comes to the cooking and housework.

"At first I resented it, especially since I was doing all of the cooking and most of the cleaning," she said. "But I don't resent it anymore, because he gives in so many other ways. He's extremely loving and supportive, which means a lot more to me than who vacuums the living room."

Gerry feels strongly that women must learn to ask for what they want and not expect men to read their minds, especially if they want to get past the first year.

"We women, particularly those of us over 40, have to learn to communicate our needs and desires. Sometimes we go the old way of being, hoping our spouses will read our minds and know what we want, or we lose our temper and start yelling. That's the old-fashioned, manipulative way of doing things. It's outdated. In today's world we need to ask for what we want, clearly and succinctly, and then see that it gets done.

"For example," she continued. "Right after our marriage, I told my husband that I need to be alone for an hour every morning to practice meditation. Early each morning, I go into my study to read and meditate and prepare myself spiritually for the day. He knows not to disturb me, but that didn't happen automatically. I had to tell him and let him know how important that hour each morning is to me and my sense of well-being. You must let your husband know right upfront what you want and what you don't want, and encourage him to be honest and direct with you about his needs."

APRIL

Adjustment takes a few months

April, the widow who remarried at 64, believes it takes a few months to work out how much time and space each partner needs.

"At first I needed more space than I need now because I had lived alone for nine years after my first husband died," she said.

"During our first year of marriage, Peter seemed to be in the way a lot. I had forgotten what it was like to have a man around all day, and at first it annoyed me, but after a few months I adjusted to that.

"We do a lot of things together, including antiquing, listening to music, and visiting friends, but there are interests we don't share and we go our separate ways for those. My hobby is sewing, his is blacksmithing. We have our own time and space for those activities. Everyone's needs are so different in this area. Just be honest with each other at the beginning and it'll work itself out."

RHODA
Above all, be flexible

Rhoda, twice widowed, lived alone for twelve years before she wed her third husband, Jules, at age 73.

"You have to learn to accommodate each other, make adjustments the first year, especially if you're used to living alone," she said. "When Jules and I married, he moved into my condo. I was upset when he wanted to make some changes. On one level, I knew it would happen, on another level, I resented it because I still thought of the condo as mine. But you can't have someone move in with you and then get upset if he wants change some things. Your home has to become his home, too.

"What used to be my guest bedroom is now his den, filled with his things," she continued. "It's his private space when he wants to be alone, and I understand that. What I've learned about being married is that, above all, you must be flexible.

"I feel I'm a most fortunate woman to have been married to three wonderful men," said Rhoda. "They were all very different in personality, but interesting and fun for each stage of my life. You have different needs when you're older—you don't have to worry about raising kids, or conflicting careers, or any of that. You can sit back and enjoy each other in your retirement years, with very little outside interference. With Jules, I hope to live in good health and peace for the rest of my life."

DENISE
Blow off steam

Denise, who remarried when she was 59, believes the secret to getting through the first year—and the rest of your life together—is feeling free to blow off steam.

"This is my third marriage and his second, and if there's anything we've both learned, it's don't bury your anger," she said.

"You must be able to blow off some steam, say almost anything and then forget it. If you air everything, then troubles don't deepen and grow.

"Another important thing is to begin marriage with the attitude that you want your husband to be as happy as he can be, and assume that he wants the same for you," she continued. "Act and react from that base and you won't be hurtful when you're busy venting your anger."

ALICE
Set boundaries early

Space and privacy are also important issues for Alice, who believes you must set the boundaries at the very beginning of a marriage or there'll be trouble ahead.

"The privacy quotient gets much higher the older you get, and the need for space becomes more important," said Alice, the one in her fifth and happiest marriage. "Be very upfront in the beginning about where you want to set the boundaries—'Don't open my mail, even if it's junk mail; don't screen my phone calls; don't go through my belongings' (if things like that bother you). All this gets more important as you get older, especially if you've lived alone for many years and are used to your privacy.

"Establish right off whatever is important to you," she continued. "If you have a daily routine that's important to you, or a hobby or special group of friends, let your husband know it. And allow the same for him. Always try to put the shoe on the other foot. Be open with each other from day one, because it's very hard to change something once it's in motion."

Like most of the women, Alice is also a strong believer in couples establishing their own, individual space.

"Space can be however you define it. It can be a separate room where you do your thing—read, watch TV, paint, sew, whatever you want to do," she continued. If you're tight on space, then carve out a separate area that's yours, where it's established that, 'This is mine, this is my area.' You can be sloppy there, or whatever, but it's OK to close the door behind you or put up a screen, or a boundary that says, 'Don't trespass.' And, of course, your husband has to be allowed the same privileges with his own space. What matters is that you have a place where you can be by yourself, do whatever you please."

Alice admits that one of the things she misses most about the single life are the long periods of being alone.

"When I'm all alone for a few hours, it's sheer heaven. I'm very happy with Brad, but I do like to spend a lot of time by myself, and he understands that," she said. "If you're like me in that respect, let your husband know at the onset of the relationship, before you marry, so he understands that it's a need of yours, not a rejection of him. Those of us who are loners at heart sometimes don't realize that people often misinterpret our need to get away from everybody and be by ourselves. They often see it as a rejection of themselves."

LENORE
Have lots of bathrooms

Space is also important for Lenore, but it took on a slightly different meaning for her when she married Jake.

"In our first house we had only one bathroom, and there were five us living there—Jake, myself, and my three daughters. He took over the bathroom, he considered it his refuge, his retreat from the rest of us, and would spend hours reading in there," she said. "If there was a true emergency, he'd get out and let one of us in, but otherwise, he wouldn't budge. If you needed to get in just to pick up a toothbrush, forget it. With three young girls, including a teenager, you can imagine what that was like.

"When we bought a new home together about five years later, I made sure we had plenty of bathrooms—where we live now we have three, so it's no longer a problem," she said, adding that he still hangs out in the bathroom, but this time he has one that's his very own.

ANNETTE
Get into the male mind

Annette, the writer who wed for the first time at 44, admits that she had a hard time the first year trying to understand how the male mind operates.

"It was hard for a while because there were things I didn't know about men," she said. "I grew up in an all-female household. I had never lived with a man. I knew nothing about how men acted. I'm sure that had a lot to do with why I didn't get married earlier.

"Sometimes I thought my husband got up in the morning and did things just to piss me off," she said. "I thought if I could smooth out those areas where he had failings, then I could smooth out our marriage. But it doesn't work that way. You're not going to change a man after you marry him."

Annette said that a friend sent her a copy of John Gray's book, *Men Are from Mars, Women Are from Venus.*

"After I read that book, I sent her a note saying, 'Thanks for saving my marriage.' I began to understand that the things my husband did that annoyed me had nothing to do with his trying to annoy me—it's just the way men are. I learned not to look at everything as something that I could change.

"One of the lessons I learned that first year was that a lot of the stuff that I argued about with Marv were things that I didn't like in myself," she continued. "I also thought that he just wasn't enlightened about some things and if I enlightened him, he would understand and these things would fall away, but they didn't."

Another recurrent theme of Annette's first year is what she calls, "Newlyweds and Menopause."

"I've heard other women talk about menopause and I've heard them talk about adjustments to marriage, and I say, 'Yeah, but you haven't lived until you get both of them at the same time,'" said Annette. "I began entering menopause just before we got married—I was having hot flashes and so forth, but I decided that it was just a state of mind and it wasn't going to cause me any difficulty, so I happily went on about my life.

"After we were married, Marv said to me, 'I really think you ought to go and see a doctor, because you never acted like this before. I've known you a long time. Your temperament usually is not mercurial. You're going off the deep edge over small things.' It came to a head one morning when he suggested I take an umbrella because it was raining, and I started to argue with him, having this big discussion about why I don't need anyone telling me I need an umbrella when it rains—I *know* when it's raining and I *know* when to take an umbrella," she said. "I suddenly heard how belligerent I sounded and finally listened to Marv and went to my physician. I got an estrogen patch, and now I'm much calmer and things are working out fine."

EILEEN
Don't mess with his stuff

Eileen and Kevin are another example of how, in practically every marriage, one person is a saver and one is a nonsaver.

Eileen considers herself a minimalist, and Kevin, according to her, is someone who never throws anything out.

"I couldn't move into Kevin's apartment until we cleared out piles and piles of stuff, including three hundred bricks that he used for a bookcase," she said. "Our first year together I tossed out a set of knives and forks from the automat that looked like junk. Kevin had found them in a flea market—he was heartbroken when he found out they were gone, and so was I when I realized how important they were to him. Since then I've been very, very careful about what I toss out, and that includes piles of what looks like junk mail, outdated newspapers and magazines. If I lived alone, I'd toss them immediately."

Can an avowed minimalist find happiness with someone whose idea of a good time is shopping, collecting, and storing? No problem. She has one closet, and a fairly empty one at that, and he has three, all stuffed. There's no competition for space.

"He loves to shop, I hate to shop. He's a clothes horse, I'm not. But it's OK, we respect each other's differences, and that's what counts," she said.

IRIS
Get two computers

It's especially important to set up boundaries when both husband and wife are retired and at home. In many ways, Iris and Michael, who were in their 60s when they married, are typical of older couples who've taken up second careers and work out of their homes.

Iris is a retired nurse who is writing a mystery novel, and Michael is a retired businessman who plays the stock market and carefully manages his own investments. Their biggest problem in their first year was sharing a computer.

"For a while we had one computer between us and it was difficult. I was trying to write my novel but didn't have any private space," she said. "Our first Christmas together he gave me my own computer and what a blessing that was. After that, I set up some boundaries because it's impossible for me to write when he's around. When I'm writing I have to be left alone. That's something he didn't understand at first. He thought he could pop in and out, interrupt me at will and it would have no effect on my concentration. I let him know otherwise, and now I have my own room with my own computer, fax, and telephone, and he has his.

"If privacy is important to you, discuss it in the beginning and set up some space for yourself," she said. "This is especially important if you work at home. Now that we respect each other's privacy things are going along beautifully."

SUSAN
Grab as much space as you can

"Sharing space? No problem," said Susan, who wed for the third time at 40. "I moved into Len's house and took over. I changed everything. My stuff is spread from one end of the house to the other."

Susan, a photographer who works out of the house, said that when she and Len were first married, he went to an office and she was alone all day. She liked it that way.

"Now he's working at home. At first I was afraid it would be a problem, but it's not because I'm in school two days a week. We each have a room in the house that we've set up as our own personal offices, and that makes a big difference in how well we get along.

"When we were first married we tried sharing a desk. What a crazy idea," she said. "He used to come to my desk and fiddle with things, or read over my shoulder. It drove me nuts and I told him so. Now he stays out of my office and darkroom unless invited, and I stay out of his office."

EMILY
Don't be his handmaiden

Emily admits that when her husband retired, having him around all the time was a real pain.

"Shortly after we were married, I quit my job to write full time," she said. "David was already retired and at home all day. Since I was no longer working outside the home, David felt he had a right to all my time. I had to let him know he didn't.

"One of my biggest adjustments that first year was feeling I had to answer to someone," she continued. "Simple questions such as 'What time are you coming home?' would drive me up a wall. I lived alone for ten years before I met David and I was used to coming and going exactly as I pleased. I didn't answer to anyone. As you get older, it's a lot harder to adjust to another person being around all the time, wanting to know about your comings and goings. The adjustment was very difficult for me.

"I go away a lot to writers' conferences without him," she said. "I also take classes and I teach creative writing for our community college. He gets upset if I'm out a lot, especially on overnight trips. He would love to have me around all day as his personal handmaiden. We work it out, but sometimes we work it out loudly."

FRAN

Tell him you love him even if he snores

Although Fran knew Craig had a bad temper, she didn't know how bad until a few months after they were married when she inadvertently turned off a talk show he was taping on TV. She also didn't realize how hard it is to live with someone who snores every night. These are the two New York writers who met at Disney World.

"He works at home a lot and uses the extra bedroom as an office," she said. "I went in there one day to use his fax machine and while I was there, I turned on the TV and flipped the channel to something I wanted to see. What I didn't know was that he had set up the VCR to record a program he planned to write an article about. When he found out what I'd done, he went ballistic.

"I always knew he could be a loose cannon when he gets angry, but I had no idea how bad it could get," she continued, "but what I've learned is that if I wait long enough, he'll apologize. That night I slept on the couch, there was no way I wanted to be in the same room with him. In the morning he apologized, as I knew he would, and I told him I was wrong to switch the TV. I've learned two things: don't touch his TV and if he blows, wait a while, it'll pass."

Snoring is another problem, one that she finds harder to handle. She said Craig snores so much that even Biscuit the cat has taken to snoring at night, something she never did all the years she lived alone with Fran.

"The funny part is, one of his selling points about himself when we first started dating was that he doesn't snore," she said. "The truth is, he snores so loud that I can hear him through the walls when I'm three rooms away. The only way I can get a good night's sleep is to get to sleep before him.

She also said he suffers from she calls Middle-Aged-Man Syndrome, or MAMS.

"You know the type, he sits in his favorite chair, immediately falls asleep and starts snoring, then he wakes with a start from his own snoring," she said.

Despite the snoring by both man and feline, and the VCR fiasco, Fran said, "I never hesitate to tell him I love him, or to tell him how good he looks when I think he looks cute, which is most of the time."

Fran agrees with the others who say that one of the secrets to a happy marriage is being good friends first.

"We just keep becoming better and better friends," she said. "I love him dearly and I know he loves me dearly, and none of the rest is really important. You can't make men fit into what you want them to be. Accept them for who they are. Appreciate the good stuff, ignore the rest. You can only train men up to a point."

It's easy to see why these women made it through the first year—they learned to walk that fine line between compromising and being true to themselves, not to mention learning not to toss out the junk he deems so precious, or carving out some space for yourself.

Listen Up

Whether you're the saver in the family or the one who clutters, the free spirit or the traditionalist, the talker or the listener, or (more likely) a combination of all of the above, you'll find the first year of marriage will make you stop and wonder how much you're willing to bend and how much you're willing to demand. Before you set your priorities, check below to see what many of the Marriage 100 consider priorities for making that first year a happy one.

Don't expect a lot of change. People are pretty set in their ways by the time they hit 40. "What you see is what you get," was the common refrain, and you'll be a lot happier if you accept that as fact. As one woman said, "Treasure his good qualities, treasure the companionship, ignore the rest."

Carve out some personal space. Whoever said, "A woman can never be too rich or too thin," should have added, "or have too much space." If you're like 99 percent of the population, you need some space of your own, even if it's the size of a broom closet. When you lived alone, you probably took space for granted. But move in with someone, especially in small quarters, and you'll find yourself screaming for some space to call your own. It's not such a big problem if you're both working outside the home, but if you're both home a lot, especially if one of you is retired, watch out. One woman, an interior decorator with a home office, married to a man who's retired and home most of the day, has a solution that works for her: She puts a skull and crossbones sign on her office door when she doesn't want to be disturbed. "You have to set boundaries and you have to do it early on in the marriage," she said. "Otherwise you've got people traipsing through constantly and breaking your concentration."

Talk things out. Just about everyone mentioned the importance of talking things out and of being upfront in the beginning of a marriage. There'll undoubtedly be a lot of differences to iron out the first year you're together. The sooner you clear the air, the better. But sometimes not talking is the best approach, according to one woman who said, "If there's a conflict, hold your tongue and think about it. Don't react right away. Try to see where it's coming from and what's really going on."

Find neutral territory. If you can afford it, make your first home together one that you've bought jointly. Each of you should sell the house you lived in with your first spouse, or where you raised your children, and move into a place that's new to both of you, and that you can furnish together. This isn't always practical, of course, but several of the women thought it was a good idea to start your life together in neutral territory. "There's a tendency to think of the house as yours if he moves in with you, or his, if you move in with him," said one woman. "Some houses have too many memories of ex-spouses or of someone else's children." Sell it if you can and move on. A fresh start never hurts.

Find time for yourself. Marriage, with or without children, takes up a lot more time than most single people realize. "Time, the difficulty of having time to myself, that was a big problem for me the first year," said one. Another said, "At first you always want to be together, but eventually you want some time for yourself, to read a book, go to a movie, take a walk, whatever. Another big adjustment for me was learning to be home with my husband without feeling we have to interact all the time."

Now that we've seen what these women have learned about the ups and downs of the first year, let's see what they propose for making the marriage last.

Chapter 10

Making It Last

Marriages are not as they are made but as they turn out.

—Italian Proverb

Just about everyone has an opinion on what makes for a good marriage and what makes a marriage last. The Marriage 100 is no exception. Those who have at least one failed marriage behind them are especially anxious to talk about why their current marriage is so much happier than their last one, and what they think helped make a difference.

I talked to those who've been married at least five years to hear what they have to say about why they think their marriages have lasted, and what compromises they've made, if any. Most importantly I wanted to find out if these women entered their current marriages feeling better about themselves. Were they really older and wiser when they picked a mate this time around? Ironically, many had first marriages that lasted over twenty years, yet they still considered those marriages "failed marriages." As one woman said, "Just because you stick together for the sake of the children, or you stay with someone because you're afraid to be on your own, doesn't mean your marriage is a success."

SILVIA AND HOWARD
Never buy clothes for each other

Silvia said the best advice she ever got on staying happily married was from the minister who presided over their marriage.

"On our wedding day our minister told us that the secret to a happy marriage is never attempting to buy clothes for each other. Thanks to him, we never have and it was the best advice anyone ever gave us." That, and their passion for politics and community work has helped them enjoy a long, happy marriage.

Silvia and Howard were married in 1966, both for the first time. They're the couple who met on a walking tour.

"I think sharing a passion for something, whether it's politics, grandchildren, or sports, is very important," she said. "I know that's one of the things that's kept us going all these years, not only as a couple, but as individuals."

Now in their retirement years, both work hard at causes promoting the welfare of senior citizens. Throughout their marriage they've been involved in health care issues, local community boards, and neighborhood associations. Saying they're active is an understatement. They're busy with Elderhostel programs, the Gray Panthers, a New York State Senior Action Council, and a public hospital community advisory board, to name a few.

Silvia also attributes their happy marriage to their mutual respect of each other's privacy and their live-and-let-live attitude toward each other.

"We don't do everything together," she continued. "I'm more interested in working with people on a one-on-one basis and Howard's more issues-oriented. We work together on many causes, but not all. We respect each other's privacy and need to do things alone, and we recognize that we each have views that the other doesn't share. You have to respect the differences in each other. Neither of us has attempted to make over the other. In any successful relationship, you need to live and let live, and it's especially true if you plan to be with someone for the next thirty years."

ALICE AND BRAD
Don't give up what you love

Alice and Brad were married in 1982. She's the mother of two who's in her fifth marriage. In many ways she's typical of the extremely independent woman who has learned to walk the fine line between enjoying lots of things alone and being part of a couple. Fortunately, with Brad she found a husband who understands this.

"I liked being single and I like being married. With Brad I have the best of both worlds," said Alice. "How? By not changing a lot of my lifetime patterns, and by not trying to change Brad. We share many interests, but those we don't share, we do on our own without any sense of guilt or hard feelings.

"I've led a very independent life. I've always been entrepreneurial," she said. "At one time or another I've owned a nightclub, retail shops, rental property, and Bed and Breakfast properties. It's what I do and who I am. If a man came along who didn't like it, that was his tough luck. That's always been my attitude and it's probably why I've been divorced four times. In my other marriages, there were times when I'd let things that were important to me go by the wayside—and that was a mistake. By letting important things slide, you're establishing a pattern that says your needs aren't important. You're giving silent approval that it's OK to ignore your needs. And that's a mistake. With Brad, I have always been very upfront about my needs and that's one of the reasons this marriage has lasted."

A good example is Alice's love of travel, which Brad doesn't always share. She let him know when they started dating that this was something she loved and had no intention of giving up.

"I've traveled alone a lot, both for business and pleasure, and I enjoy it," she said. "When I take a trip alone, Brad knows I'm not going somewhere to meet other men, I'm going on my own because that's how I am. A pleasure trip doesn't have to revolve around the opposite sex. You can sit and talk to men and not have ulterior motives. Brad and I both give each other complete freedom to socialize with the opposite sex. That freedom is very important to both of us.

"But that's just us. Other couples might not feel so loose about it. The important thing is that you let each other know what's important in the beginning. If you try it later, you will end up with major problems," she said. "I think this is true of any relationship, whether it's a friendship or a marriage. Certain things have to be established in the beginning to avoid problems later."

Alice believes strongly that it's important to be yourself, from day one.

"You must be who you truly are, but in a way that's palatable to the other person," she said. "And, boy, that's a challenge."

One example she gives is the different ways she and Brad handle problems in public.

"I'm terribly outspoken, Brad is a typical, New England WASP who thinks it's only the ill-mannered who show anger or strong displeasure in public," she continued. "If we're in a restaurant, for example, and something's wrong with the food, I'll send it back. Brad would die first. He was raised to believe that it's bad manners to send food back. If you're married to someone like that, you still send the food back, but you do it in a quieter, more discreet way than if you were alone. Issues like that come up with us all the time.

"Brad has to get angry to take action, I don't," she continued. "To stay with the food metaphor, you must send it back if something's wrong, because that's the type of person you are. If you don't, you won't like yourself—and you'll also ruin a good meal. By the same token, if it's Brad's dish I don't interfere. It's his call. I have to admit I have a hard time holding my tongue in a situation like that, but I do. I know Brad would rather eat an overdone steak or a tough piece of veal than send it back—there are a lot of people like that and you have to respect their position."

Alice feels that the main differences between older marriages and younger ones is that as you get older you realize that no one person can validate who you are.

"When we're younger, we're foolish enough to think that one person can cover all the bases for us, we think he'll be our lover, our friend, our confidant. Maybe it happens sometimes, but it's rare," she said. "I think the older you get, and if you've been married more than once, you start to know this instinctively. You're happy as long as the majority of the important bases are covered. And even if all of the bases are covered, you still have to work at knowing yourself and being your own person, because relationships are constantly shifting and changing."

Despite Alice's independent nature, she still believes it's important for couples to have some interests in common. For her and Brad, that interest is art.

"Art has been one of my major interests for the past few years, both as an artist and as a student," she said. "When we were first married Brad didn't have much interest in art, so I pursued it on my own. Recently he took up woodcarving as a hobby and that led to his developing an interest in all types of art. Now we both really enjoy going to art galleries together and taking art classes."

SUSAN AND LEN
Go off on your own sometimes

Like Alice, Susan thinks it's important to go off on your own once in a while. She feels absence definitely does make the heart grow fonder and it's a shame that most couples don't allow themselves some time apart. Susan was married in 1993 at age 40.

"It's very important to take a breather from each other now and then, especially if you're having problems and you're at an impasse over a particular issue," she said. "Walk away for awhile—be alone or with a friend, but be sure it's someone who will let you be yourself."

Susan said during her first year of marriage to Len, they had a strong disagreement about something and fought about it a lot. One day she left and went to her mother's for the night.

"Mom was a three-hour drive away," said Susan. "As I was driving, I started to think and I began to clear up the cobwebs. I wasn't running home to mom, I didn't even discuss the problem with her. I didn't need to because the long drive helped me understand what was wrong, and being away from Len helped me be more objective. By the time I got to my mother's, I had pretty much worked out the problem and then I was able to relax and simply enjoy being with my mother.

"I'm lucky, I have a wonderful mother—she never pries, she didn't ask why I was there or what was wrong," said Susan. "She knew I would tell her if I needed to, but I didn't need to, so we just enjoyed a pleasant, relaxing evening together and I left the next morning feeling refreshed and in control of my situation."

Susan said it can also work the other way, especially if you're alone in your house.

"Sometimes, when Len's away on business for a day or two, I can feel the emptiness," she continued. "If we've had a fight, I realize that the things I said in a heated argument weren't all that important. Other times I wake up in the morning and am happy he's not around, at least for a while."

STELLA AND CARL

You must have similar values

Stella, the schoolteacher, wed Carl in 1973 and credits their long and happy marriage to two words: similar values.

"You must have similar values if you're going to be happy with someone," said Stella. "For me, it's basic. If a man's overriding interest is making a lot of money and he's going to spend all his time working to make money, be sure you share those values," she said. If you don't, if you like a comfortable life but have other goals besides being wealthy, you're going to resent your husband's focus on money and his workaholic ways. It doesn't mean your values are superior to his, it just means that it's too big a gap to bridge."

Stella credits shared values for keeping this marriage on an even keel, despite some stormy seas.

"Carl is an artist and he has the temperament to go with it," she said. "He's tempestuous and impulsive. I, on the other hand, am very controlled and organized, almost to the point of being compulsive about it—it's led to some stormy times. But what helps see us through the bad times are our shared values and shared interests. Neither of us cares that much about money, beyond our having enough for a reasonably comfortable life. But I share his love of art and we both love to travel, we both read a lot, we have the same political viewpoint and we love to discuss and interpret politics and world events."

What interests don't they share?

"He collects catalogues of every description, and reads them from cover to cover. He enjoys cooking, I do not, so I let him do most of the cooking," she said. "I enjoy shopping, he hates it. That's about it."

Lenore and Jake
You must compromise

Just about every woman mentioned the importance of compromise.

"You *must* be willing to compromise if you want a lasting, happy marriage," said Lenore, who married Jake in 1975. "For example, I like a neat house, it makes a difference to me. My husband doesn't care about neatness. He's a saver. He saves every last piece of paper that goes through here. I don't dare throw anything out, because only he knows where important papers are buried, or where to find things he thinks he'll need someday. I used to nag him about it at first, but it only created tension. Now I accept it as long as he keeps the mess in certain corners of the house. It's a compromise on both sides. You have to do this with every issue. Don't think it ever ends—it doesn't."

Lenore also said that you should never stop expressing love and affection for each other.

"We have very deep feelings for one another," she continued. "We both feel that each is the other's half. At least once a day we say, 'I love you' and do a lot of hugging and kissing. We're very affectionate with each other. We hug hello and good-bye, we hug each other when we pass in the hall, we show affection for each other any chance we get. I know it sounds corny, but it works. After you've just hugged someone, it's hard to start nagging him because he left the newspaper scattered all over the floor."

Lenore also thinks that in any marriage, it's important to develop a thick skin for those inevitable cranky moods.

"When he comes home tired and hungry, and he does it a lot, he starts picking on me, trying to rile me," she said. "It used to really upset me and I'd take everything to heart. Not anymore. I know the crankiness stems from fatigue and hunger and that as soon as he sits down and relaxes a bit, and then has his dinner, he's fine. If I argue with him before dinner, it only makes matters worse.

"My mother taught me to never pick an argument before or during dinner. If you have a complaint, wait until afterwards. You'll both be more mellow by then," said Lenore.

ANNETTE AND MARV
You'll always have baggage

Annette, who wed Marv in 1990, believes you have to constantly work on yourself to keep a marriage going.

"One of the biggest challenges is dealing with the baggage we bring into a relationship," she said. "It's hard to do it without professional help, but you can do it on your own if need be. It's something you have to constantly strive toward, no matter how long you've been married.

"My history includes abandonment issues," she says. "My mother died young, my father left us, I went to live with an aunt, then with a grandmother. So I have this fear of abandonment that gets in the way sometimes. Marv, on the other hand, has real problems with people raising their voice at him. I haven't been able to put my finger on where that comes from (and he hasn't said) but a raised voice indicates very negative kinds of things to him. If you shout, he will clam up.

"You have to constantly be aware of your feelings and when you fall back into old patterns, say to yourself, 'This is a new situation and my response is completely inappropriate for the current situation.' I have to continually remind myself of this—it's become my mantra.

"Sometimes, too, we have totally different ways of dealing with disputes or disagreements," she continued. "If you disagree with me, you have to tell me why. You may or may not be able to persuade me, but you can't just let it go. Marv thinks when I do that, I'm being argumentative, but I'm not, I'm just trying to understand."

Holly and Jack
Don't let him retire

When you marry later in life, sooner or later you're going to have to face the problems of his retirement, which means he's around all day. For women who work at home and are used to solitude during the day, coping with a husband who's home all day can be a major headache. Holly, who married at 43 in 1973, is going through that now. When she sold her real estate business, she started a second career as an artist. Her husband, an engineer who retired five years before her, is having trouble finding what to do with his time.

"Men should never retire. They don't know what to do with themselves," she said. "At first Jack played golf a lot and read books. Now his health is bad, so he can't play golf and he can't get out much. He's become the 'checker,' as in, 'Are the lights turned off? Is the washing machine off? Who is that on the phone? Who is that letter from?' I think this comes from sheer boredom. Men should work until they drop in their boots. So should we. I am not about to sit on my butt." And she doesn't. In her 60s she went back to college and earned a B.A. and then became an "encaustic" artist, employing an ancient Egyptian technique that involves burning colored wax onto wood panels. Holly set up a studio in a shed in their backyard and goes there every morning, blowtorch in hand.

"Jack respects my privacy while I'm in there, but the rest of the time, forget it. If your husband is retired and you're both home all day, you must find some space of your own, where you can put up a 'Keep Out' sign," she said. "If we didn't have a shed, I would probably have rented a small studio because it's impossible to get anything done with your husband breathing down your back."

Laurel and Daniel
Share the same religion

"My husband and I are still very romantic and crazy in love," said Laurel. She and Daniel were married in 1993, the third time for both of them. She was 40, he was 50. Both say their religion plays a big role in their marriage.

"Our spiritual beliefs are alike and we feel they are the foundation of our marriage," said Laurel. "We feel God is in charge of our lives and that he will never give us more than we can handle. If there's a problem or a crisis, we both deal with it from a spiritual perspective. We believe every problem comes with a blessing or a gift, even if it's not immediately apparent.

"These shared beliefs help us in all areas of our lives. If one of us felt this way and the other didn't, it would be difficult, especially when things go wrong."

Holly and Jack also believe that love and marriage know no age, no prejudice or limits of any kind.

"At 40-plus, love and marriage are fabulous. Maybe because by the time you reach 40, you've had enough experience to know what's important and valuable in life," she said. But she cautions against thinking you can sit back and relax.

"A happy marriage is a process, not something static," she said. "You're constantly shifting, adjusting, and compromising. Where you find your comfort level is an individual thing, and what's comfortable today may not feel comfortable tomorrow."

Arlene and Jim
Have a common outlook

Arlene, like Laurel, says having the same spiritual beliefs is very important in a marriage. For her, having the same religion means having a common language. She wed Jim in 1993.

"We share a common belief system, a language we each use to comfort one another in tough times," she said, adding that this marriage is much happier than her first marriage, which lasted twenty years.

"Jim and I are both better people," she continued. "We've both been married once before and we've learned from our mistakes. For one thing, I no longer need marriage or a man in my life to enhance my self-image. And we have a spiritual bond, which neither of us had in our first marriage."

JOYCE AND KEN
Climb those mountains together

In 1988 when Joyce, the couch potato, married Ken, the athletic type, little did she know that 'Climb every mountain' would be more than just a song to her.

"Thanks to Ken, I've learned to enjoy outdoor exercise and I've even climbed mountains with him, something I would never have done on my own," she said. "It's very important to have a lot in common and make an effort to get involved in each other's interests if you want your marriage to last.

"I share many of Ken's interests and it has enriched my life. If you don't have much in common, then the relationship probably isn't going to grow. Ken and I share the same values, we enjoy the same lifestyle—I didn't have that in my first marriage. I made sure it was there with Ken before I decided to marry him."

Joyce said she's also developed an interest in the financial markets, thanks to Ken, and now she's not only full of energy, but she's financially savvy, something that gives her a lot of self-confidence.

Like so many of the other women, Joyce puts a lot of stock in the ability to compromise.

"With all you're getting, get more flexibility," she said. "You must be willing to look at your husband's point of view and be willing to accommodate differences of opinion and different ways of doing things. Who says we become more set in our ways at we get older, we can do the reverse. The choice is ours."

She said it's also important to prioritize, to put the relationship ahead of always expressing your anger.

"When you're having a bad day and you want to scream at him, ask yourself whether venting your anger is worth hurting him. No matter how mad you are, slow down, stand back, look at the overall relationship," she said. "Try to keep your focus on good things that happen in your marriage. If you're still angry and feel you must express yourself, then do it in a calm way with a minimum of hurtful words."

Joyce is another who puts religion high on her list of ways to keep a marriage happy.

"More and more I think religion is very important in a marriage," she said. "We're both Episcopalian. I'm more involved in church than he is, but we share the same spiritual beliefs and we go to church together."

BEVERLY AND MATT
Be open and honest

Beverly is one more who believes that open communication between a husband and wife is one of the keys to a lasting marriage. To this, she would add friendship and teamwork. She married Matt in 1991 at age 50. It was the third marriage for both of them.

"What makes this marriage different from my other two, both of which ended in divorce, was the fact that we are open with one another, we communicate our feelings, and we are relaxed with each other," she said. "We know that neither of us is perfect. I think a lot of this comes with maturity, which you rarely have the first time around."

SHARON AND ED
Don't strangle each other

For Sharon, who married Ed in 1993 when she was 53, mutual respect and space top the list of how to keep a marriage going.

"Without mutual respect you have nothing. It encompasses everything, it allows you each to have your own space," she said. "We both work out of our home, but in separate rooms. He's an accountant, I'm an antiques dealer. We need the separate offices to keep from strangling each other. We respect each other's space and privacy—I don't step foot in his office without invitation, and he does the same for me."

EMILY AND DAVID
Don't be each other's clone

"What makes a marriage last? Keeping in mind who you are, and not becoming a reflection of your partner," said Emily, the one with the doberman, who wed for the third time in 1990. "Also, you must have a certain level of independence, write your own checks, have your own credit cards, along with some independent activities. For example, I read for the blind one day a week, without him, and he plays tennis with friends, or sits alone playing computer games, two activities I'm perfectly happy to pass up.

"You need shared interests, too," she continued. "It doesn't have to be everything, but enough to create a bond," she said. What they do share is a love of golf, beach walking, food ("I cook, he eats"), card-playing, and being with their grown children and grandchildren.

RITA AND LARRY
Say "I love you" a lot

"Larry tells me every day how much he loves me," said Rita, who married for the second time in 1985. "He has not missed one single day. My first husband never said, 'I love you.' Those are three very important words to say and to hear on a daily basis.

"Most women learn their mistakes from their first marriage, especially those of us who married young, before we really knew what we wanted out of life," she continued. "One of the most important lessons I learned from my first marriage was that you cannot remold a man to suit yourself. You must accept who he is and if you don't like everything about him, work around it."

Rita also believes a couple must trust each other totally.

"There is no jealousy in our marriage," she said. "We trust each other completely and we do nothing to cause any distrust. Your marriage won't last without trust, whether it concerns finances or the opposite sex."

Monica and Ted

Get a housekeeper

Marriage is sharing and caring, but it's also biting your tongue, slamming the door behind you, and taking lots of deep breaths. At least that's the opinion of Monica, an artist who wed for the first time at 44 in 1991.

"We lived together for a year before we decided to get married and I thought I knew all there was to know about Ted," she said. "But things that didn't bother me much the first year we were together began to really get on my nerves about halfway through the second year of our marriage. Some of it was cumulative, like his heavy smoking. The more I read about the dangers of second-hand smoke, the more convinced I became that his disgusting habit was going to kill me someday. Another was his sloppiness, always leaving the newspapers strewn all over the floor, his dropping dirty socks and underwear next to the bed rather than putting them in the laundry hamper. I entered the marriage knowing this about him, but it really started to bug me in our second year."

She realized that one of the reasons these things were bothering her after their marriage, not before, was that until they wed, she rented a small studio several miles from home where she went off to work every morning. Now she works at home.

"After we were married, we bought a rambling old house with plenty of room for my studio, so I started working at home," she said. "It was seeing the mess during the day that was getting to me. Also, he's a salesman and works out of the house a lot, and I felt he was breathing down my neck all the time."

She solved one of the problems by getting a housekeeper to come in once a week.

"Here I was resenting the housekeeping, resenting picking up after him, resenting taking time from my work to wash the dishes, when all I had to do was hire someone to do those things for me," said Monica. "If you're going to fight over who scrubs the floor, or you're going to resent his sloppiness, hire someone else to take care of it, even if it means cutting back elsewhere. Believe me, a good housekeeper is worth every penny."

She's still working on some of the other problems—his smoking, for example.

"He's honestly trying to quit, and he's definitely cut down," she said. "My getting angry only made matters worse because the anger just caused him to reach for another cigarette. He knows I love him, even if he does smoke, and he knows I want him to quit so we'll be able to grow old together without a lot of medical problems brought on by smoking.

"Over the years we've learned to talk things out, to try to work things out together, not just to act like spoiled brats wanting our own way," she continued. "What a difference it makes when you discuss problems calmly without accusing each other of being in the wrong. I think that's something that only comes with maturity."

GLADYS AND RAUL

Don't let a disability stop you

"Unconditional love, that's one of the biggies," said Gladys, who wed for the second time in 1989. "Don't marry someone and think you'll change him. You can only change yourself."

When Gladys speaks of unconditional love, she knows what she's talking about. She has MS, a disease that has slowly weakened her since her marriage, but the bond between herself and Raul remains as strong as ever.

"When I met Raul, the disease had progressed to the point where, when I was tired, I'd drag one foot. I told him on our first date that I had this problem," she said. "He thought it was temporary but I told him it wasn't and that it would get worse. By the time we married one year later, the disease had progressed to the point where I was using a cane. Now I'm in a wheelchair 96 percent of the time."

She said they've both adjusted to her condition and Raul has become very involved in the local MS Society.

"Raul is on the same wavelength as I am, as far as our handling of the disease is concerned," she said, adding that disabled people shouldn't assume they can't find a loving partner.

"I hope that people with disabilities don't give up on finding someone special," she said. "The person they marry would gain a lot from that relationship. A caregiver, if it's the right type of person, would not see it as a burden. With Raul, helping me is an effort of love, and I would wish someone like Raul on any woman, disabled or not."

As you can see, there are lots of opinions on what makes for a long, happy marriage. Age is obviously not a handicap. In fact, judging from some of the comments of the Marriage 100, youth can be a definite handicap when it comes to picking the right man and getting your priorities straight. Collectively, they can look back on plenty of broken marriages and disastrous relationships, all entered into before they had the wisdom and maturity to know better.

Listen Up

Here are ten ways, not necessarily in order of importance, to make your marriage last, according to the Marriage 100. Most of the women admit they learned these lessons the hard way.

1. Communication is the key. Knowing how to communicate and talk things out is very important. Practically all of the women listed the lack of good communication as one of the reasons their previous marriages failed, and they credit good communication as one of the prime reasons for their current marriage succeeding. As one woman said, "There's usually not enough talking in a relationship. Communication is a major skill. Those who don't communicate have a lot more trouble in their marriage." Another said, "Before you marry, be certain your future husband is willing to talk things over. So many men in their 40s and 50s just never developed the ability to express their feelings." But communication doesn't just mean knowing how to express yourself, it also means knowing how to be a good listener. That may be the most important of all.

2. Find some space and privacy. It seems the older you get, the more you need space and privacy. This was especially true of women who've lived alone for a long time. For some, space and privacy means a room to yourself, where you can shut the door on the world (and your husband); for others, a few hours to yourself out in the garden or at the local library, or hanging out at the health club. But all agreed it has to be give and take. One woman said, "If you're both retired and at home most of the day, it's essential you establish some rules, otherwise you will drive each other nuts. If you're trying to work out of your home or pursuing a hobby that takes a lot of concentration, for sure he'll drive you nuts, always looking over your shoulder to see what you're doing, or interrupting you because he wants something. You must say, 'This is my time, this is my space, stay away.'"

3. Be each other's best friend. Many of the women mentioned that their husband is their best friend. "We are each other's best friend," said one woman. "We discuss everything, we confide everything in each other, we do everything together." While not all the women said they were *that* close to their husbands, just about all of them mentioned that they and their husbands were friends first, lovers second. Many felt that a deep friendship was *the* most important quality in a happy marriage. "Sex was great while it lasted," said one woman, "but it sort of tapered off. What we have now is a friendship that means much more to us than sex ever did." Another said, "Look for a man who'll be your friend and give you lots of emotional support. That's much more important than financial support." Another said, "What's the point of getting married at this stage in your life unless he's your best friend?"

4. Learn to compromise—a little. Everyone agrees it's good to give and take. But as one woman who wed at 45 said, "You must walk the fine line of making this relationship work without giving up what you've spent years building." Another said, "Compromise when necessary, but don't compromise on anything that's really important to you or you'll end up resenting it."

5. Develop shared interests. You don't have to do everything together or share every interest, but if you don't have some interests in common, you're probably not going to stay together for long. Three of the women said they and their husbands did everything together, another said they didn't do anything together except meet for dinner and discuss their day, and they both liked it that way. The majority, however, were somewhere in between, with five or six shared interests and about the same number of interests that they pursue on their own.

6. Similar values. Just about everyone agreed that you need to have similar values, or you're in trouble. For some this meant the same religion, but for most it simply meant wanting the same things out of life, having the same basic goals. Some liked going out to dinner a lot and traveling, others enjoyed staying home and pursuing hobbies together. Some are big spenders, others thrifty. There's no right or wrong, there's just harmony or trouble. As one woman said, "Opposites may attract, but they seldom stay together."

7. Toss out old baggage. "It's hard to let go of past bad habits but you have to if you want your marriage to last," said one woman. He needs to dump old baggage, too, according to another, "In particular, he should be committed to examining and eliminating deep-seated male chauvinist attitudes."

8. Be yourself. "Establish your own identity and don't ever give it up," said one woman. Another said, "Before you marry, learn what makes you tick, what's important to you. Don't fall into those destructive, outdated ways of living through your husband—they don't work for the long haul."

9. Be upfront. Have important issues decided and discussed *before* you wed and you'll have fewer problems later on. Put it all on the table—how you want to handle finances, your kids, his kids, future kids, whatever is important to both of you.

10. Live and let live. "What you see is what you get" was the prevalent attitude of those who've been married awhile. "The best part of a mature marriage is that you don't have to try to change each other, you don't have to prove anything, you can relax and enjoy one another as is," said one woman. Another said, "No young children, no money problems, time to enjoy each other. That's why older marriages are happier."

So there you have it—the collected wisdom of one hundred very honest women, women who wish you the same happiness most of them have found and who leave you with one special thought: Go for it!

Appendix

Here's a sample copy of the questionnaire that I sent to the women who would eventually become the Marriage 100. Their interesting (and often impassioned) answers to these questions led to hours of telephone conversations with many of them and, eventually, to this book.

Marriage Questionnaire

Note: Your real name will not be used
(Please type or use pen)

For longer answers or additional thoughts, please use reverse sides of the paper or additional sheets of paper. Remember to include the number of the question.

Name:
Address:
Home Phone:
Office Phone:
FAX:
When is the best time to reach you?
Do you want to be called in your office or at home?

1. Date of current marriage:
2. Your age at the time:
3. Your current husband's age at the time:

4. Is this your first marriage? His first?
5. If no, how many for you? How many for him?
6. Your age in previous marriages: His age:
7. Length of your previous marriages:
8. Length of his previous marriages:
9. Times widowed: , times divorced: (You)
   Times widowed: , times divorced: (Your husband)
10. If previously married, how long were you single between this marriage and the last one?
11. Number of children (yours), if any, from previous marriages:
12. Age and sex of your children from previous marriages:
13. Age and sex of his children from previous marriages:
14. Age and sex of children from current marriage:
15. Age and sex of grandchildren (yours and his combined):
16. Age and sex of children (or other relatives) living at home:
17. Your occupation (if retired, give your occupation prior to retirement):
18. Your husband's occupation:
19. Are you retired? Yes No
    If Yes, for how long?
20. Is your husband retired? Yes No
    If Yes, for how long?
21. If you're not retired, what are your retirement plans, if any (e.g., move to a condo in Florida, travel a lot, do volunteer work, golf, etc.)?
22. If you are retired, how do you and/or your husband spend your time?
23. How did you meet your husband?
24. Were you looking for a mate at the time? Yes No

25. If Yes, please explain why (e.g., lonely, looking for security, wanted to share, etc.), and what you did, if anything, to meet men:
26. If No, please explain why (e.g., liked single life, involved in a career, child-rearing, burnt out, etc.):
27. How long after you met your current husband did you have your first date?
28. Type of date:
29. What was your initial reaction to your future husband?
30. How soon after your first date did you decide to marry?
31. Did you live together first? Yes No
If Yes, for how long? Do you have an opinion, pro or con, on mature couples living together before marriage?
32. If either of you have children, what was their reaction to your plans to wed?
33. Reaction of other family members:
34. Reaction of your friends and co-workers:
35. Reaction of your women friends:
36. Describe your wedding:
37. What advice would you give women 40 or older who would like to marry or remarry?
38. If this is not your first marriage, how does it differ from your previous marriage(s)?
39. How important is sex in this marriage?
40. List the three most important qualities you think 40+ women should possess to attract eligible men:
41. List the three most important qualities you think women 40+ should look for in a prospective mate:
42. Do the qualities you listed in #41 differ from what you looked for when you were younger? Yes No
If yes, please explain:

43. What does your husband say attracted him to you?
44. What qualities in your husband attracted you?
45. What interests, hobbies, etc., do you and your husband share?
46. Which of *your* interests do you not share with him?
47. Which of *his* interests do not interest you?
48. Does religion and/or spirituality play an important role in your marriage? Yes No
    If Yes, please explain:
49. Describe yourself: Weight Height Hair Color
    Eye color Race and/or Ethnic Group
50. Do you work out at a gym or engage in any form of regular exercise? If Yes, please describe:
51. Describe your principal home (e.g., house, condo, rental) and give approximate size:
52. If you have vacation homes or other homes, please describe:
53. Describe your community (e.g., suburb, small town, large city, etc.):
54. Did you read (or were you aware of) the *Newsweek* article that said a woman over 40 had a better chance of being kidnapped by terrorists than of marrying? Yes No
55. If Yes, what was your reaction?
56. Is there any other facet of *your* marriage that you would like to discuss when we talk?
57. Is there any facet of the marriage over 40 issue that you would like to discuss?

Thank you for your help and cooperation!

Please list names and addresses of other women you know who might like to be part of this study:

____

____

____

____